Free Indeed

Free Indeed

❧

ESCAPING BONDAGE AND BROKENNESS FOR FREEDOM IN CHRIST

Dr. Richard Ganz

Free Indeed ©2002 by Richard Ganz

ISBN 0-9723046-3-0

Unless otherwise noted, Scripture quotations are from the New International Version (NIV), ©1994 International Bible Society. Italic text indicates emphasis added.

Cover design by Tobias' Outerwear for Books – www.tobiasdesign.com
Cover artwork by Nicora Gangi – www.machairastudio.com
Interior design and production by Andrew MacBride

Manufactured in the United States of America

To Dr. Jay E. Adams, who has dedicated his ministry to teaching that the Bible is sufficient for Godly living. I thank you as well for the simple truth that seemed so revolutionary back then: "You are competent to counsel one another." Romans 15:14

Contents

Acknowledgements		IX
Foreword		XI
Preface		XIII

INTRODUCTION		1
CHAPTER 1	*Freedom True and False*	6
CHAPTER 2	*Freedom: Internal versus External*	8
CHAPTER 3	*Freedom, Psychology, and the Church*	11
CHAPTER 4	*Freedom and Slavery*	15
CHAPTER 5	*Freedom from the Expectations of Others*	17
CHAPTER 6	*Freedom to be Your Own Person Before God*	22
CHAPTER 7	*Freedom to Move Beyond Self-Imposed Limitations*	27
CHAPTER 8	*Freedom to Fail and Succeed*	30

CHAPTER 9   *Freedom to Love*   34

CHAPTER 10   *Freedom to Change*   37

CHAPTER 11   *Freedom in Deed and Thought*   42

CHAPTER 12   *Freedom and Emotion*   45

CHAPTER 13   *Freedom from Self-Love*   49

CHAPTER 14   *Freedom in Denial, Cross-Bearing and Following Jesus*   53

CHAPTER 15   *Freedom Now*   59

CHAPTER 16   *Freedom to Serve God Rather Than Self*   67

CHAPTER 17   *Freedom from Demanding Our Own Rights*   70

CHAPTER 18   *Freedom from Holiness*   75

CHAPTER 19   *Freedom for Holiness*   80

CHAPTER 20   *Freedom and Law*   83

CHAPTER 21   *Freedom And The New Life*   91

CHAPTER 22   *Freedom to Remain Shackled: Its Consequences and Costs*   99

CHAPTER 23   *Freedom In Joy*   105

CHAPTER 24   *Freedom from Hopeless Bondage to Sin: A Case Study*   108

CHAPTER 25   *Freedom: Responsibility versus Sovereignty*   115

CHAPTER 26   *Freedom and Conspiracy: Man's Quest for Personal Freedom*   119

CHAPTER 27   *Who is Free?*   125

Conclusion   130

Acknowledgements

I am thankful to Professor Harold Harrington, the Dean of students at Ottawa Theological Hall for checking the book for sound theology. I am also grateful to Dr. Jay E. Adams and Rev. Matthew Kingswood for doing the original editing. My friends Stu and Kathy Schmidt and Alaisdar and Eleanor Graham provided energetic support for this and other projects of mine through the years. Stas Jesionka has always helped with his artistry and creativity. The cover art work is by Nicora Gangi. I am honored that her magnificent work should grace the cover of my book.

I especially want to thank Rick Irvin and Aaron Tripp of Shepherd Press. They are incredible publishers and a real blessing to work with in the production of a book.

I want to thank my wife Nancy and our children Shoshannah, Elisha, Natanyah, and Micaiah. I Praise God for the support and encouragement of a loving family.

Finally, I want to thank God for taking me and extricating me from the bondage to and love of sin, and making me instead to be "Free Indeed" (John 8:36).

Foreword

*E*very once in a while, a really wonderful book comes along. This is just such a book. Once you pick it up, you won't be able to put down. In this book, Rich Ganz takes on one of the most important issues in the life of a Christian: freedom. In doing this, Dr. Ganz fills a void that desperately needs to be filled. There is nothing in print that has looked as carefully at this subject. It is a subject that touches every person on this earth. It is especially necessary in counseling, where enslavement is the norm. Every Christian counselor, indeed every Christian, should read this book. Drawing from his almost thirty years of experience as a biblical counselor and pastor, Rich shows how Christians can have the freedom that Christ gives his people. You, like me, are going to find this book to be one of the most encouraging and helpful books you have read in a long time. If you read only one book on counseling this year, this should be it!

I worked with Rich for five years at the Christian Counseling and Educational Foundation. During this time he demonstrated tremendous skill and insight as a biblical counselor. That same energy, passion, and concern comes through in his book.

I recommend this book as highly as I can! I am very glad that Dr. Ganz has provided this helpful and valuable tool for the desperately needy counseling ministry of the Christian church.

I am sure that God's people will be incredibly blessed as they apply the applications of the principles in this book. Use it devotionally. Use it in Bible Study groups. Use it in Sunday schools. In whatever way you use it, you will receive the blessing promised by Christ: "You shall be free indeed."

Dr. Jay E. Adams

Seminary professor, Biblical counselor, pastor, internationally renowned seminar and conference speaker, and author of many books on Biblical counseling.

Preface

Free versus Free

I grew up in the 60's. If there was one quest we all had back then, it was a quest for freedom. We wanted to be free, and we looked for heroes. The problem was that we didn't really have a clue where to look, because we were in bondage to sin. Everyone we looked to only deepened our death sentence. I looked to Abbie Hoffman, the leading radical of the 60's. I was fascinated when he caused a riot in the New York Stock Exchange by throwing hundreds of one-dollar bills into the air. I was entranced when he led the student demonstrations at the 1968 Democratic National Convention. But I was finally hooked when he changed his name to "Free." Then the years passed. I was converted and grew into a strong believer in Jesus Christ... And Free...

He died. This man-of-many-names, who once led the nation's youth in its quest for freedom, could not escape the shackles of death. Abbie Hoffman lies imprisoned in the grave. He could call himself "Free," but the grave finally constrained him. He was a symbol of the Sixties and a general of that generation. "With one hand waving free, silhouetted by the sea,"[1] he rode that wild wave of liberty as if it would never hit the shore. But it did.

What was that wave? Even those who were carried along by it did not understand its turbulence or exuberance. How could such a profound revolution begin in such a simple fashion? "Hair! Hair! Hair! Hair! Shoulder length or longer!" I remember the day I joined the rebellion. For years Scotch Tape and Dippety-Doo had held my curls down, but then I raised the flag of my revolt against the establishment: I let my hair spring free! Why? As our poets sang to us,

> Almost cut my hair
> It happened just the other day
> It was gettin' kinda long
> I coulda' said it was in my way
> But I didn't and I wonder why
> I feel like lettin' my FREAK FLAG FLY . . .[2]

Raising that flag was just the beginning. The fight for freedom (in what Hoffman termed a "revolution for the hell of it") meant challenging every standard and crossing every boundary. "Do it!" was the yippie war cry. The removal of all restraints (both internal and external) was the goal. Even the biochemical structure of one's own mind became a barrier to be broken. Normal perception became a constraint to the exploration of inner space. The doors of perception were unlocked. "Expand your mind" was the new slogan. "Do you remember what the door-mouse said? Feed your head!"[3] Drugs fuelled the flights over the borders of reality. Yes, reality itself was viewed as an arbitrary imposition and restriction. As our prophets sang to us, "Nothing is real and nothing to get hung about . . . strawberry fields forever."[4] But strawberry fields were not at the end of that fast lane free-way, and the ancient prophets who warned of disaster were ignored. "There is a way which seems right to a man, but in the end it leads to death" (Prov. 14:12).

Once before in history, a man named himself Free. It was

Martin Luther. The name Luther means "Free," and he understood it literally because Jesus Christ had set him free from the
bonds of sin and death. Abbie Hoffman and Martin Luther had
opposing views of freedom. While neither was willing to be in
bondage to any man or any human institution, freedom for Free
Hoffman meant breaking every boundary; for Free Luther it
meant discovering, understanding, and submitting to the boundaries created by God. For Hoffman, being free meant to defy all
authority; for Luther, it meant to submit to Almighty God, the
One who had legitimate and ultimate authority . . . even over life
and death. Hoffman's final act of defiance was to take his own life,
thereby affirming that he was autonomous, free to determine his
own death. For Luther, defiance itself had to die so that he could
live. Freedom was not achieved; it was granted. Luther stumbled
upon a strange paradox: When he bowed his knees and surrendered his life to the LORD, there was freedom! His signature on
a "declaration of dependence" meant liberty for him, forever! In
losing his life, he had gained it. Jesus Himself said, "So if the son
sets you free, you will be FREE INDEED" (John 8:36).

God alone (not the most compelling revolutionary) can
give this benediction to His people: YOU SHALL BE FREE.

Endnotes

1. "Mr. Tambourine Man." *Bringing It All Back Home.* Bob Dylan.
   Warner Bros. Inc., 1964, 1965.
2. "Almost Cut My Hair." *Déjà vu.* David Crosby. Crosby, Stills, Nash,
   and Young. Atlantic, 1970.
3. "White Rabbit." *Surrealistic Pillow.* Grace Slick. Jefferson Airplane.
   RCA, 1967.
4. "Strawberry Fields Forever." *Magical Mystery Tour.* Lennon/Mc-
   Cartney. The Beatles. Capital, 1967.

Study Guide

1. Find someone who grew up in the Sixties. Try to find out
   what made freedom such an important issue to this person.

2. Martin Luther and Abbie Hoffman both sought to be "free," but they understood freedom differently. What did each seek freedom from? What did each seek freedom for?

3. As a Christian, what would your own "declaration of dependence" affirm?

4. Jesus promised "you shall be free" (John 8:36). How has he fulfilled that promise in your own life?

Introduction

*L*ong ago, the Rabbi Saul of Tarsus, known later as the Apostle Paul, said something extraordinary: "It is for freedom that you have been set free. Stand firm then, and do not let yourselves be burdened again by a yoke of slavery" (Gal. 5:1–2). Jesus anticipated the significance of this claim in His own teaching. In His first public address, He declares that He has come to "proclaim freedom for the prisoners . . . to release the oppressed, to proclaim the favorable year of the Lord" (Luke 4:18–19).

The theme of this book is freedom in Christ in daily life. Its purpose is to help you experience the full freedom His salvation offers.

Yet the freedom Christ talks about is sadly lacking in His church. There should be no creature on earth more free than a follower of Christ. Yet it is my observation that the church, behind its stained glass windows, its creeds and confessions, its testimonies, and what can become cheap clichés ("praise the Lord," "Amen") is a body of conflict-riddled, burden-bearing, guilt-filled, miserable creatures, more worthy of pity than emulation. Some of these poor creatures have been persuaded to believe that they must express joy and freedom in Jesus with pasted-on smiles that look like someone shoved a clothes hanger into their mouths. The tension for them in living a Christian life is enormous. In some Christian circles, to drop the smile is tantamount to admission of defeat. In others, believers are taught to continually experience the miseries of worthlessness as a kind of antidote against pride—which, of course, it can never accomplish. True humility comes only when we see ourselves accurately, not when we make ourselves miserable or ecstatic according to some preconceived notion of Christian piety.

I have been a Christian for over thirty years now. While I made no bargains in coming to Christ, I did not commit myself to Him in order to experience inner ruin and trampling. My initial experience as a believer was the honest exhilaration of having the promise and expectation of eternal life. Meeting other believers was a signal for joy. I assumed that they had seen their privileged position, as I had, and renounced the self-defeating habits and hopes of their old way of life. Every minute of life was a moment to be cherished as a gift from God, to be used for His glory. This was what I understood at the beginning. Soon I began to realize that other Christians did not experience their life in Christ in the same way. Festering beneath clouds of piety was bitterness, jealousy, anger, and complaining, all of which I had known before coming to faith in Christ.

My trust in Christ continued, but two regrettable things resulted:

1. I became distrustful of other Christians. I began to expect (albeit unconsciously) a kind of pettiness and meanness surrounded by mock piety. I came to expect hypocrisy.
2. My own experience of living began to deaden. As I accepted the cultural and ecclesiastical norms as biblical, I began surrendering my freedom in progressive ways. Jesus remained real, but everything else took on a shade of unreality. The

core issues of Christianity became blurred. It became increasingly difficult to know what "living by faith" really meant. When the expression "he lived by faith" was used, it usually meant that he was not so carnal as to actually receive a salary for a daily job. Or, perhaps, that he refused to buy life insurance or health insurance.

How long will God's people be so ignorant of the freedom they have in Christ? Paul said he was "free from all men" (1 Cor. 9:19 NASB). That doesn't mean that we owe them nothing (we owe them love!), but simply that we are not under their crushing judgment. The only judgment that matters is God's judgment on our sin, which Christ has received on our behalf. The destruction of biblical freedom disintegrates the vibrancy of the Christian life.

In my case, slowly, indeed imperceptibly, I began to move away from my first love, a love that filled me with courage, confidence, and freedom. I moved from the middle class to the "Christian" middle class. I moved from the world of the guilt-racked infidel to the world of the pious pretender. I lived by the values of my new peers and again slipped under the crippling tyranny of man, only now in the name of God. I say all this as a confession, not as an attack. My desire is that Christ's people will drop all their self-defeating defenses, their extra-biblical inflexibilities and instead:

1. Come to God in humble dependence upon Him and His grace, find, and practice the freedom He has given us in Christ.
2. Come to His Word, appropriating it and living it in joy, instead of forcing it to fit our own pre-Christian prejudices.

I want to see God's people set free from their crippling estrangement from personal relationship with Christ and brought into deeper fellowship with Him, a fellowship in absolute truth. Jesus declared, "I am the truth" (John 14:6) and that, "the will shall set you free" (John 8:32). The truth is infallible because He is the truth. I am concerned that we have misinterpreted that truth and turned it into bondage.

My basic presupposition is that Jesus Christ is truth, and He gives freedom. Thirty years ago I came to the realization that Jesus is the truth, and so concluded that unswerving obedience to Him is essential. I have sought to honor that commitment, but only recently have I understood and experienced what His freedom means. We must be as deeply committed to exercising that freedom as we are to believing in the truth.

That does not mean that freedom is set against truth. The Christian who accepts full freedom in Christ is not isolated from people, or from himself. He cannot use Christ as an excuse for being nasty, selfish, or unloving. The free man in Christ wears the cleansed robes of Christ's righteousness (Isa. 61:10) and daily experiences new mercies (Lam. 3:22–23) from which flow gratitude, love, sacrifice, and obedience. The free man in Christ is what Paul calls the "bond-slave of Christ." He belongs fully to Jesus, and this is his freedom. He doesn't just "live for God." He lives passionately for God. He is alive. Every moment is precious because it is an opportunity to feel the pleasure of God's presence.

This book is for Christians. While I hope that many who are not Christians may read it and be drawn into the freedom found in fellowship with Christ, my principal goal is to reach Christians who hunger and thirst after the meaningful life of freedom in Christ that they never seem to attain. It is for all who stumble and fall, who think they can't get up but hate lying there. It is for those who have squandered their lives living everyone else's expectations but have never lived their own calling in Christ. It is for those who have fought for freedoms but still are not free.

It is my prayer that this book will help God's people become what they are meant to be in Christ: FREE!

Study Guide

1. If Christians are "free from all men" (1 Cor. 9:19), why do we still tend to submit ourselves to others' judgment of us?

2. Are you a pious pretender? What two approaches does the author suggest to move you toward deeper, more authentic fellowship with Christ?

3. A Christian wears the "robe of righteousness" (Isa 61:10) purchased by Christ. What other "robes" do you tend to put on to try and please men?

I

Freedom True and False

*F*reedom is not unlimited choice. Society is crumbling because people are living as though freedom means the rejection of all external restraints. Restraint is linked with inhibitions, and in an age of permissiveness, no one dares to admit to inhibition. As long as freedom is defined by inner determinants—urges, sensations, drives, and desires that one "must" express—chaos will ensue.

Society has abandoned the notion of objective metaphysical or spiritual truth. How strange this is! In science, which has become modern man's religion, only what can be objectively measured is considered open for investigation. Values, being intangible, are not scientifically knowable, but are considered purely subjective and personal. Only what one feels or experiences has worth. In this view there are no guiding laws or principles, but there is one absolute. That absolute is that there are no absolutes. You are the captain of your own ship. The new freedom is complete autonomy, but it is an impossible goal. And even if autonomy were attainable, is it desirable? All around us we see people adrift on a sea of limitless alternatives, and the consequences are devastating. Like sailboats without rudders, they drift, lose control, and inevitably capsize.

Standing opposed to this is Christian freedom. This freedom is internal and external, both in our thought life and in our actions. Christians do not act as though people are autonomous. God establishes our freedom within boundaries. We are free to make choices. We are free to follow an external standard, or we may choose to make our own whims our standard. But choices have consequences.

The question is: What kind of freedom will we choose? What consequences are we prepared to accept? Will we choose a freedom that has no fixed values to guide it? Or will we choose a more blessed freedom that guides us into an abundant life? Will we look to the One who created human life to reveal the way to us? Ultimately, this freedom to choose the life we were made for is the only freedom that counts.

Study Guide

1. What kinds of chaos ensue when we define freedom by inner desires, drives and urges?

2. Have you ever noticed that "there are no absolutes" is an absolute statement? If this thinking is all around us, how might it have influenced our own thinking?

3. Christian freedom is based on the fact that the God who created us knows the best way for us to live. How is this different from seeing humans as robots?

4. How might Christian freedom be both "inner" and "outer"?

2

Freedom: Internal versus External

*C*an true freedom coexist with external, fixed standards? Our society condemns the externally guided individual as the unfree individual. He is viewed as someone who avoids responsibility for his actions and/or emotional state by placing it on someone or something external. The moral person in our society is internally controlled, having no outside standard. This idea of morality appeals to people, but it makes the gigantic assumption that all that is necessary to make optimal choices lies within the individual! While it seems attractive, it places each person alone on that uncharted sea of which I spoke in the last chapter. There is total responsibility, but no ultimate meaning. An inner resolution to destroy would be as good as an inner resolution to create.

This view avoids the fact that we can never escape the countless external influences impinging upon us. When we deny that reality, it removes us from the most significant influences of all: God, Law, and Revelation. All this is done in the name of our supreme freedom, but in reality it is only the freedom to despair.

So if we reject the idea of purely inner direction, does that mean we are externally controlled? More directly, does belief in a living and personal God who acts in history mean that he is externally controlling us?

Let me suggest, first, that personal freedom is not so easily obtained, simply by determining one's own personal values. Rather, our choices are inevitably the product of countless conscious and unconscious interactions with the world. The real issue is determining who will help us make our choices by their instruction and example. Once we understand that, our entire frame of reference changes. If we choose to believe God, we are not alone. Through Christ, we are in the deepest of all possible relationships, that which the Scriptures call a "covenant."

What I am suggesting, therefore, is that freedom is the inescapable outcome of two worlds in interaction: the internal and the external. Freedom involves an inner choice and an external, or transcendent, value. As humans, we experience life both subjectively and objectively. To make choices we should first gather all of the significant available data. Everyone does this, to varying degrees. The supposedly internally directed individual, presupposing the uselessness or unavailability of such data (values, objectives, etc.) external to the self, utilizes little of what is available. He chooses amidst seemingly limitless alternatives and stands heroically in the assertion of absolute freedom. Such individuals suppress the reality that they do not exist in a random, impersonal universe (Rom. 1:18). They deny the truth that their lives are not only given, but sustained, by a loving Creator/Redeemer God (Rom. 1:20). They are aware that the profound choice they face (whatever it may be) involves intense personal responsibility, but their choice is no more "ultimate" than they are. They deny that God, rather than choice, is ultimate. This is true even if in their mistaken idea of freedom, they crown choice as god.

Strange as it may seem, it is precisely because God is ultimate that we are free to choose, and to experience the attendant emotion and consequences. This is God's world; He has supremacy over all things. We are free to succeed and free to fail because our goal is neither success nor failure, but to live according to the standard of God.

How unfortunate that Christians do not clearly see how great their freedom in Christ is! God's standard does not destroy the responsibility of freedom, but deepens it. True freedom is realized every time a believer attempts to choose, perhaps contrary to self-interest, what will glorify God! Of course, this does not give us an alibi for not living in the fullness of the joy which God has provided. If we fear God's freedom and opt out of obedience, that choice is evil, for it exhibits lack of trust in God. This sin (lack of trust in God) permeates the contemporary church.

The church is not trusting God. How can her individual members be free? Let us consider, then, the church as an agent of freedom in Christ.

Study Guide

1. Consider some of the many external influences and limitations on your life, and how they impinge on your ability to exercise unlimited "freedom." How does this fact humble you? How does it bless you?

2. How does the fact that God not only created but sustains every human being affect the way you make decisions?

3. Why is the glory of God a greater goal than our individual successes or failures?

3

Freedom, Psychology, and the Church

Sad to say, the church is more an agent of modern psychology than of Jesus Christ. The church has tended to adopt secular models, and the present is more or less a baptized psychological model. It has done this hoping to bring joy and freedom to man. Why? Because the church, like the world, sees the psychologist as the primary agent of personal change, rather than its pastor/shepherds. In doing so, the church has rejected the God-ordained means of accomplishing these things. This is a dangerous road to travel, because it denies that God and the Bible are able to bring freedom and joy into the lives of believers.

A real sleight of hand is necessary to accomplish this. Instead of seeing man as a material and spiritual unity, it becomes necessary to divide man up into parts: mind, will, and emotion. Each of these parts is thought to act independently of the other. Instead of seeing that the Word of God brings complete restoration, psychology is called in to help fill a supposed void. The result is a further fracturing of man, making joy and freedom even more difficult to experience.

This fracturing of man lessens what man in totality is. Reducing man to mind, will, and emotion compounds this error, and then focuses upon one particular aspect of man, depending upon which segment is under observation at any particular time. Such fragmentation never tells what is really happening to a person, any more than a physician really possesses a complete picture of what is happening to a patient by looking at one organ system without observing how the symptoms are affecting the person in his entirety. When the church exalts either mind, will, or emotion over the whole being of man, a number of serious errors may occur:

Mind. The segment of the church that gives pre-eminence to the mind sees its religious worldview focused on knowledge-seeking. Religious life is reduced to intellectualism, becoming obsessed with abstractions regarding doctrinal orthodoxy. This often amounts to salvation by cognitive knowledge of the truth. But the Scriptures always demand more than mere knowledge of truth. James condemns the error this way: "You believe that God is one. You do well; the demons also believe, and shudder" (James 2:19 NASB).

Will. In giving religious pre-eminence to the will, this segment of the church assumes that we are dealing only with the moral nature of man, his will to do right or wrong. This view is erroneous for two reasons. First, if religion is morality, then if you keep the Law, you are saved. Paul explicitly denounces this view as anathema in Galatians 3:10. Second, it reduces the religious life merely to doing good, i.e. works, which is ultimately no different than the first.

Emotion. Romantics reduce religion to feelings. The whole Romantic movement was a reaction to intellectualism. For the Romantic, the way to find truth was to get in touch with your feelings. Obviously, emotionalism is still pervasive both in our culture and in the church, to epidemic proportions. As a religious phenomenon, it is closely allied to Mysticism, asserting that God speaks to individuals through their feelings. To be saved, then, it is only necessary to "feel" saved. This seems to be at the heart of neo-orthodoxy and many of the "neo" religious groups that have sprung up in this century. God, they say, communicates salvation directly and bypasses the intellect and the will. This type of subjectivism is deadly for believers. Yet it has an understandable starting point. Many Christians have long been disgusted with the mere intellectualism (mind fragmentation) or legalism (will fragmentation) they observe in much of the church. Individuals who are drawn to the more emotional or mystical parts of Christendom "feel" (and to a certain extent they are right) that the knowledge of God involves far more than abstract intellectualism or diligent action.

Neo-Pentecostals substantiate their religion of feeling by claiming mystical ideas of revelation in which God speaks directly with them (but often without words), bypassing the will and the intellect. This fragmentation owes its origins to Liberalism with its roots in the preaching of Schleiermacher, who appealed to the feelings while discarding the Word of God.

Any view that sees man as only one aspect, as opposed to a unity, will lead to a truncated and distorted Christian life. It will never facilitate true Christian freedom, because it is a distorted view of man. It is rare to see a church teach the true and complete interdependence of all of these aspects of man. Some churches believe this theologically, but still send their parishioners to secular psychologists.

Of course the full freedom we desire will not simply appear when mind, will and emotions are integrated, but when man, in his totality as a religious being, grows in his covenantal relationship with God. In other words, man is truly free only as he lives entirely devoted to communion and fellowship with God. Only then, in his freedom as a reconciled image-bearer of God, can man use his intellect passionately as a responsible moral agent. This produces a church free of the bondage of intellectualism, emotionalism and legalism.

1. Why do you think the church is drawn to secular psychology? What past failures of the church have made psychology so appealing? What does psychology seem to promise that would draw us away from Biblical truth?

2. The psychological approach divides the unity of man into mind, will, and emotion. How does this division conflict with a Biblical understanding of human nature?

3. What is the difference between knowing God and knowing about God? What are some consequences of a purely intellectual faith?

4. Read Galatians 3:10. If no one can be saved by keeping the law, how does this shape our understanding of the human will?

5. Which aspects of human nature are bypassed in the Mystical view of emotion? Why is this view so dangerous?

4

Freedom and Slavery

*B*iblical freedom is always expressed in contrast to bondage. It is also seen as both freedom from something and freedom for something else. Thus neither freedom nor slavery function alone; they are correlative states. As we have already seen, freedom is a central biblical construct. "It was for freedom that Christ set us free" (Gal. 5:1). Writing to the church at Rome, Paul repeatedly contrasts this freedom with the believer's former slavery.

In the sixth chapter of Romans, he declares that the grace and liberty we possess can never be a license to sin. This is because our freedom in Christ brings with it a definitive break from sin. This break is so profound that Paul says we who are in Christ "died to sin" (v. 2).

To reinforce this separation from a former life of sin, Paul goes on to say that not only are we dead to sin, but being dead, we are freed from sin. Without this freedom we would be still alive to sin; that is, sin was the reality principle by which we lived. We were "slaves to sin." But freedom in Christ is so profound that Paul declares we are "set free from sin" and have now become "slaves of righteousness" (v. 18). Or, as he puts it later in the chapter, "slaves of God" (v. 22). This slavery, he goes on to say, enables you to "derive your benefit, resulting in sanctification, and the outcome, eternal life" (v. 22 NSAB).

This truth slices through every man-made notion of utter autonomy and unlimited choice. Biblical freedom is enslavement, but enslavement of a new and deeply benevolent kind that issues in holiness and life. This is the message that our world, buried under the rubble of its notion of freedom, desperately needs to hear: that it has been enslaved to sin and self all along. Paul deals with the consequences of such enslavement: "The wages of sin is death" (verse 23). But he also shows the way out: "The free gift of God is eternal life in Christ Jesus our Lord." This free gift is what makes us truly free, giving us eternal life to be lived in Christ Jesus our Lord.

Study Guide

1. Christ delivers us from slavery to sin and death, but then leads us to become "slaves to righteousness" (Rom 6:18). What is the difference between these two kinds of slavery?

2. What two benefits of slavery to God does Paul mention in Romans 6:22?

5

Freedom from the Expectations of Others

I lived at home in New York City until I was twenty-one, when I graduated from the City University of New York. After graduation, equipped with a generous U.S. Public Health Fellowship, I was off to the great unknown (Detroit, Michigan) and my career as a doctoral student in clinical psychology. As I was preparing to leave with both suitcases, my mother cried out, "Is this what I raised you for—to leave me?!"

This is known as a Jewish guilt trip. My mother believed she had every right to lay this on me. She was very Jewish, very much my mother, and very good at manipulation. I was prepared to respond as I always did at such acute moments when my own feelings of guilt soared. I would shriek at her, she would shriek back at me, and before long, we would be embroiled in a wild accusation-exchanging free-for-all. Her favorite retort was, "You won't be happy till you hammer the last nail into my coffin!" Eventually I would experience a true sense of guilt that I might indeed be causing her death by my actions. Statements like hers, when heard thousands of times in a person's life, can effectively manipulate him to live out someone else's expectations and aims. For twenty-one years I had responded in ways that consistently confirmed my mother's assumptions.

So there we stood on that eventful day in June, 1968. The big question had been posed: did she have the right to assume that I would live according to her expectations? You would think I could see through such nonsense, but I was as blind as all others who willingly fall into the "manipulation trap." When we live according to the expectations of others, we fall prey to this kind of manipulation. The great tragedy in all this is that there is always another way out. 1 Corinthians 10:13 reminds us that God will always provide a way out. These ways are almost always simple, and would keep us from experiences that are painful and damaging to all parties involved.

What is heartbreaking is that most individuals have never tried these biblical tactics. Their lives are a mess. They live according to others' expectations, rather than God's. They allow themselves to be improperly and unbiblically guided.

This is not to say that there is never a time when we can be correctly directed by others. The problem is not that we may be satisfying other people's expectations. The problem is that we do this to fulfill what others think they need. Yet a correct response that is other-directed may go against what the other person says he or she wants.

It is important to live your life by standards you uphold for yourself. We all adopt certain standards, both consciously and unconsciously. Even when we adopt the standard that there are no standards, this is a standard. It is wise to acknowledge this fact, because it keeps us from spending our lives in reaction against every one and everything. We can live at peace with people even when our decisions have gone against those who are important to us. Our aim is not peace at any cost, but rather to serve God all the days of our lives with all that we are. This attitude will often make you exasperating to others. In this respect Jesus is prototypical. Even at the age of twelve, His mother, seeking Him, finds Him and asks, "Where were you?" (i.e., "You were not where I expected you.") His response was, "Didn't you know I would be about my Father's business?" He is doing what He is meant to do, which presents a real choice to those He loves who have very real expectations for him. They can continue to ply their expectations on Him (useless) or modify their expectations according to the person they behold in front of them (useful).

Most individuals foist their prejudices and expectations upon the people who are important to them. The result is often that they meet with the rejection of these expectations and are left confused, hurt, and angry. Often these same people have not yet learned how to disassociate and differentiate themselves from their important people to become persons dependent only upon God. Thus, they live as automata.

They are addicted to slavishly meeting the expectations of others. They are paralyzed by the thought of taking action on their own and assuming personal responsibility. How often does God, or the devil for that matter, get blamed for their own sin-filled cowardice and slavery to the expectations of others? They choose to live by the myth that one day they will be free of some circumstance or person (a mother, by the way, can go with you even when she's dead). One day everything will fall into place and they will:

1. Be who they're meant to be.
2. Be who they want to be.
3. Do what they want to do.

What a myth! In fact, the reverse is true. It ends like it begins. A society of automata will die in shackles. By contrast, a truly free individual can't be shackled even by chains. Perhaps this is why the rich and powerful always seek to chain a person who is truly free. What a threat he is! By his life he declares to them: "You are not free." His life declares that freedom is not external but deeply internal, in spite of any material blessings.

Can you begin to comprehend what it means to be free

from the expectations of others, free to be uniquely yourself? This is always good when we choose righteously! God, having created us in His image, never meant our freedom to be an excuse for wickedness. Our uniqueness, and our joy in it, must be found in our ability to love, never to harm. Freeing yourself from externalized expectations that are wrong allows you to love those you used to hate, who held something over you. Their hope-filled expectations made you feel enslaved and helpless to extricate yourself. In your slavery, you didn't realize that freedom was right around the corner.

You can choose to respond according to the expectations of other people, or you can respond according to what you believe is right as you take everything biblically significant into consideration. So if you respond according to the expectations of other people, don't hate or develop bitterness towards them. It's not their fault. You don't have to respond in such a manner. You are free to respond very differently. But oh, how safe it is to blame someone else for your anger or depression! It saves you from taking responsibility for your life and actions. "He drives me crazy" is much easier to say than "I make myself frenzied and anxious every time I am with him, because I am afraid of standing up to him, lest he withdraw his approval." Let's go back to my mother and her question. Had she raised me to leave her? "Yes, Mother! That is precisely what you raised me for! To leave you!" All that wasted energy! All those stupid guilt-trips! All those bizarre screaming sessions! What if I had succumbed? May God have mercy on those who live out, not their own lives, but someone else's. They are like ghosts, walking dead. Their lives have ended and yet they continue. They present us with some of the greatest tragedies of life.

Yet even for them there is hope. God is not thwarted by domineering Jewish mothers (or any other kinds of parents, friends, or whomever). He can turn even a walking dead person into a child of God and give him a new birth, with a new life and a new walk. How good God is! Living for Him is the antithesis of living for others. It is freedom. All our drives, talents, and resources are put to full use. He now makes us what we are meant to be. Here's to your freedom!

Study Guide

1. Can you tell the difference between true guilt and a guilt trip? How do you distinguish between God's standards and the expectations of others?

2. 1 Corinthians 10:13 promises that God will provide us with a "way out" when we are tempted. How might you take this way out when someone tries to manipulate you with guilt?

3. Jesus dealt with the expectations of others by doing his Father's business. What is the Father's business in your life? How might remembering God's priorities for your life help to distinguish them from others' expectations?

4. We tend to live by other people's expectations because we think we'll get out from under them eventually. Why is this a myth?

5. Think about how much of your time and energy goes into meeting the expectations of others. Now consider several ways that God could use that time and energy to transform your life according to his expectations!

6

Freedom to be Your Own Person Before God

*T*his theme is closely allied to the preceding chapter. The person free from the expectations of others is free to be his or her own person before God. This is genuine freedom. Most people have no idea who they are, where they're heading, or why. More and more young people today choose to be motivated by job concerns (which are real concerns), but at the expense of their own interests, gifts, and other personal considerations. People feel real pressure and expectation to choose their life's work (and commit themselves entirely to it) before they have much real experience in life! Of course, experience isn't absolutely necessary. Knowledge of life is what is necessary. Knowledge comes by experience, but it can also come by authoritative instruction.

The priority now is to get a job, not to discern God's calling. With an attitude like this, whatever job you ultimately get will remain alien to your basic character and personality. If young people went into the working world with a sense of religious calling (i.e., viewing work as a service to God), talented entrepreneurial people would choose many different directions. Products wouldn't be so crassly material, but rather, those things which, while bringing satisfaction and happiness, would also serve some spiritual ideal.

This concept of calling may seem to undermine the profit motive. Material profit is not always unspiritual, but profit (under any circumstance) must not become one's god. Only the Lord is God. Think how much the structure of our economy would be altered by people making uncoerced choices. There would certainly still be pressure, but to which pressures does one give his attention? Personal freedom is not the absence of inner constraint, but a realistic awareness of our motivations and the ability, in light of this knowledge, to do what is honoring to God regardless of the cost.

This means exercising the freedom to say "no" to what is dehuman, de-personal and destructive. This means at times going against friends, peers, family and colleagues. You may be alone for a long time. It may be difficult. It is hard to choose integrity above camaraderie. Being your own person before God involves an economic reality, and that can produce struggles. Yet for most, seeking the approval of their significant others is of greater importance than the economic factors, and brings even larger battles into their lives.

Many people willingly give up their own values, morals, goals, and lifestyles for the approval of significant people in their world. What a sad choice! The people to whom they succumb will not likely accept them anyway. People who use others rarely give of themselves, even when others sacrifice to please them. Much of this discussion is crystallized by the question, "Will I work in the system, outside the system, or around the system?" If you choose to work around the system, it will soon catch on to you and conclude that you are an outlaw. You will have alienated everyone. You will not be approved by those who demand that you work in the system, nor by those who recognize that you are an outlaw. You will also forfeit the respect and approval of those who admire the person who has the courage to follow his own convictions.

Have you ever asked, "Do I really want to do what I am doing?" Doing what we want to do is never the final criterion for anything. However, I am concerned that most people are so out of tune with themselves that they have no idea what they want. That is how strong approval-oriented behavior is. Jesus put it so well: "What does it profit a man, if he gains the whole world and loses or forfeits himself?" (Luke 9:25 NASB). You think you will profit from such behavior, but you will lose. Your loss is yourself.

"Do I really believe this is right, or am I just doing this because it is expected and will gain external gratifications?" This question presupposes that we live in a world of absolutes, that there is truth and falsehood, good and evil, right and wrong. Being your own person before God means that you acknowledge God. He is the standard of right and wrong. Being your own person in this sense is not being autonomous, but making your decisions according to the revealed will of God.

Everyone has some standard. Even if you are always in flux and completely dependent on the situation, why should you trust a "situation" to reveal a solution? Why should you trust it more than the commandments of an absolute and holy God? Being your own person is not becoming an individual who looks within for answers. Being your own person is having the confidence that God has given you the knowledge of right and wrong and the courage to act rightly, amidst all contrary pressures. This is not the kingdom of self. It is not license to do your own thing at the expense of others—some of whom, perhaps, you once begged for approval. On the contrary, Christianity claims a revelatory model of right and wrong that the child of God should follow. As he follows this designated path, he sees his character more and more molded and restored into the image of God.

This image is found by looking to Jesus, the Author, Perfecter and Leader of our faith. What we have in Jesus is not balanced behavior but proper respect for God. Jesus never succumbed to the pressures around Him. For example, Peter said he would never let Jesus die. Fully knowing His own course, Jesus said, "Get thee behind me Satan." Pilate demanded that Jesus speak, suggesting that such behavior might save His life. Jesus responded, "You would have no authority over me unless it had been given you from above" (John 19:11 NASB). Jesus affirms here the absolute sovereignty of God, a sovereignty that allows him to choose a hideous death because it is God's will.

This is our example of self-controlled but responsible behavior towards God. It involves both an existential and a theological perspective. Both must be reckoned with in any mature or godly understanding of Christian freedom.

In other words, both the situation and what God says must be taken into account as we become honest with our lives before Him. You cannot just look at the situation in which you find yourself, or your own inner pulls and subjective experience. These are important, but the whole picture must include the theological element; that is, what God has to say about our actions in this kind of situation.

Freedom to be your own person before God involves responsibility as a Christian. As we have seen in the example of Jesus, one freedom can often cancel another freedom, such as the freedom to live. Perhaps we should make a distinction between Freedom and freedoms. A person can give up freedoms and remain Free. Jesus was Free on the cross, yet he chose to lay down many freedoms or rights (e.g. walking about, breathing, and living). What was at stake was Freedom. Freedom must not be lost, even if all freedoms must be sacrificed.

We can see this distinction in everyday life. People in a broken relationship with God invariably assume that they can attain freedom. But the Scriptures speak of a Freedom that is not attained; it is a gift. That does not mean that one should be discouraged from seeking freedom, but simply to see that it cannot be bought with silver or gold, or merited by any worldly accomplishment.

Nor is Freedom just a state of mind. If this were the case, all who felt free would be free. Freedom is not a feeling. Jesus was most free as He affirmed His destiny in Gethsemane, while dreading the scathing destruction of the cross. Freedom to be your own person before God demands looking yourself squarely in the face, according to the will of God, without hiding or fear, and taking the required steps regardless of where they lead. It is not loving yourself or this life more than Christ. This is part of what Jesus means when He speaks of "denying self." The cost of Freedom is the denial of personal freedoms that stand in the way of true freedom.

Study Guide

1. Have you experienced the tension between merely getting a job and discerning God's calling? What's at stake in the direction you take?

2. In what areas of your life do you have a difficult time saying "No"? How can saying "Yes" too often impinge on your freedom in Christ?

3. You are called to be your own person before God. How can you live this way without drifting into human autonomy? What smaller "freedoms" might you need to give up in order to be truly free?

4. Meditate on the suffering and death of Jesus Christ, who gave up his freedom and yet remained free. If this is what it cost for God to give you freedom, how important is it for you to exercise your freedom in obedience to him?

7

Freedom to Move Beyond Self-Imposed Limitations

*L*et us move from the conceptual to the practical. If people do not know what freedom is, then they do not know how to live freely. There are many ways in which we choose to enslave ourselves. A common way is by setting limits, which we will never risk going beyond. Fear grips us. We picture all kinds of frightening scenarios that paralyze our freedom to act. We fear we are unable to go beyond what we assume we are. Yet there is almost nothing quite so freeing as taking even a small step that changes what we previously thought unchangeable:

> "I will never be able to read."
> "I will never be able to control my anger."
> "I will never be a good student."

Most often these kinds of comments come from individuals who assume they have no hope of personal growth. They look wistfully at others making strides in life and assume there is no possibility for them to do so. Their problem is that they look at the result rather than the process. They see only the success, not the steps leading to it. They chalk success up to genetic factors: "That's just the kind of person he is." Rarely do they ever consider the choices, self-control, and hardships involved in attaining great accomplishments. It is quite amazing how most people content themselves with a life of little or no growth, fearing to test their own limits lest they lose the little they have.

I am not talking about encouraging a person who is eighteen years old and 5'3" tall to try to become the center on the university basketball team. I am talking about unrealistic, self-imposed limitations, not God-imposed ones. You cannot make yourself tall or short, or become a professional football player at age fifty-five. But you can conquer the host of self-imposed and imaginary limitations. You can test and accomplish your potential if you are willing to use all that you are as an image-bearer of God—a full and free individual.

How? First of all, recognize what you are doing. If your life lament is "I could never even dream of doing that," you are denying your freedom. Many people have a bad experience or a lack of success at some point in their lives. From that point on, they base their actions on that remembered failure. Every new venture is immediately associated with remembered hurt. They have never learned how to go beyond these strong associations to create new ones.

Second, you must identify the behavior(s) you would like to acquire, e.g., self-control, good study habits, etc.

Third, you must list everything you see standing in the way of success, e.g., "That lousy T.V. is such a distraction . . ."

Fourth, you must specify everything that would help you have a breakthrough. "Boy, if I just had a quiet room."

Finally, you must prayerfully begin to implement some of the changes.

The exciting thing is that as you start doing these little things, you are making changes and the more changes you make, the less you will view yourself glued into a fixed role. Your life is increasingly freed up to discern and evaluate the influences upon you. You become free to make changes consistent both with who you are and who God wants you to be. In the process, you become much less oriented to the idea that you are what you do, e.g., "I am an accountant." Instead, you are thinking and involved in the joy of living, in which you continually test your gifts and calling, in faith, without fear of failure or inordinate lust for success.

For most people the shackles are not simply "I could never be an accountant," but rather, "How horrible it would be to fail." Is it horrible to fail? What is failure? What is success? We will now take a radical look at success and failure and our great freedom to succeed . . . or fail!

Study Guide

1. What do you fear?

2. What is the difference between God-imposed and self-imposed limitations?

3. The author suggests five steps to take you beyond self-imposed limitations. Walk through these five steps with one of your own self-imposed limitations.

4. If Christ gives us freedom to fail, how might this affect our worldly labels that suggest "What you are is what you do"?

5. What might the life "job description" of a Christian look like? How does this description provide both guidance and freedom?

8

Freedom to Fail and Succeed

A number of years ago I took my family to Europe. The purpose was to write a film script. The project failed miserably, and our lives were shaken dramatically. My wife and I deeply experienced a profound failure. During this time, a friend of mine said something that revolutionized my thinking. He asked, "Do you still have your faith?" and instantly I shot back: "Of course. It's stronger than ever." He responded, "Then how can you see yourself as a failure?"

We must all establish what we believe is the true criterion of success or failure in life. Society has its standards for success, most of which are the very things Jesus condemns as ultimate goals for our lives. They include affluence, or the ever-expanding accumulation of things and money. They also include careerism, or getting jobs just for the jobs they will lead to. A relative of mine once said, "You can still make something of your life," observing that I was a pastor instead of pursuing a private practice in clinical psychology and psychotherapy, in which I am trained and licensed.

Jesus declared, "Do not store up for yourselves treasures on earth, where moth and rust destroy, and where thieves break in and steal. But store up for yourselves treasures in heaven, where moth and rust do not destroy, and where thieves do not break in and steal. For where your treasure is, there your heart will be also" (Matthew 6:19-21 RSV).

We have become a society conditioned by the approval of others. We let others define success and failure for us according to man's standards and not God's. We remain under terrible bondage, selling our true freedom to exploit gifts that will be used to attain someone else's ideal. How ironic it is to have everything society deems valuable and at the same time be miserable! Yet this is the plight of most people. From childhood on, we are conditioned to look to others for definitions of acceptable gifts and callings.

I once spoke to a young man with an obvious interest and skill in philosophy and the humanities. I was saddened when he told me that he was going into electronics because "that is where I can get a job." Should this have troubled me? Isn't it an understandable attitude? Or should we not appreciate that the foundational basis for work is the mandate from God to go and subdue the world for Him and for His glory (Gen. 1:28).

Our post-Christian consensus denies not only God's mandate of work, but God Himself. And denying God leads to hatred of work. So we take our place at what we acknowledge as a worthless task for the paycheck and what it will buy. We suffer our job for the security it gives, as though we really are capable of controlling our future! It reminds us of the biblical parable of the wealthy farmer who looks out only for his future financial security, longing to be able to say "I have ample goods laid up for many years" (Luke 12:19). But Jesus concludes, "You fool! This night your soul is required of you."

Within this context, men give away their future and their present. They sell their lives for a job. They give up the dream of a calling to do something worthless. They are not free. They go home, not to continue in their work and to train their children in work, but to settle into the easy chair of a life of slavery, selling out to the devil for the price of worldly comforts. If ease is the goal, they are at least partly successful. But is this success? Can they convince themselves it is? Do they wonder, "Is this all there is to life?" They pursue success with a vengeance, but it always eludes them.

The Christian is meant to be free. His freedom allows him to succeed or fail with little grave difference to his peace of mind. This is because the challenges in his life are deeply personal and internal, not external. He does everything "with all his heart, as for the Lord rather than for men" (Col. 3:23). He knows that his "labor in the Lord is not in vain" (1 Cor. 15:58). Thus, in faith he cannot fail.

I do not mean that everything done in faith is inherently acceptable to God, as if it could not be designated as failure or sin. The reason that what is done in faith does not condemn (Rom. 14:23) is only because Christ has died for our sin. Rash or imprudent people should not take comfort from my words. But if a believer does fail according to the world's standards, he can take it in stride if he has been faithful to God and obedient to His commandments. He knows that the Lord is with him. There is always the joy of striving with all your might at those things you cannot fully master, articulate or even comprehend. There is satisfaction in the calling to which you have given everything, even if you see no fruit yet. This was often the plight of the prophets in the Old Testament.

Remember this: Part of your calling is to give all you have to it. You are free to succeed. You are free to fail. Success can be almost as difficult as failure, but don't be ruined by either. Neither success nor failure is your goal. Your freedom extends to something much greater than this, to which we now give our attention.

Study Guide

1. Consider how many of the things you invest your life in are earthly, "where moth and rust destroy" (Matt 6:19–21).

Where are the "heavenly treasures" in your life, and how can you invest in them?

2. Why does denying God lead to hatred of work? How does acknowledging God lead to a redemptive view of work?

3. Our society is obsessed with earthly security, and Christians often fall into the same trap. How can we live in a way that trusts only in eternal security without becoming so heavenly minded as to be "no earthly good"?

4. The apostle Paul encouraged believers that their "labor in the Lord is not in vain." (1 Cor. 15:58). How might this verse help you when you fail, or when success is not immediately apparent?

9

Freedom to Love

*I*t is possible to assume that freedom is our goal. This is nonsense. Freedom should no more be a goal than happiness. Freedom is the by-product of life rightly lived. Freedom doesn't make failure less painful or success more exhilarating. Freedom allows us to dare. The most daring activity and the true goal of man is to love. Yet even within the fulfillment of our responsibility to love, we all fail.

Love doesn't look to itself but to the other. Love is not weak. It is not some emotion-ridden excuse for hedonistic self-pursuit.

If one is not free in Christ, he is not free to love. When Jesus was confronted by the question, "Teacher, which is the greatest commandment in the Law?" (Matt 22:36) he answered without an instant's hesitation, "'You shall love the Lord your God with all your heart and with all your soul and with all your mind.'… And the second is like it, 'You shall love neighbor as yourself'" (Matt 22:37, 39).

Consistently and persistently seeking the best for another, even if by sacrifice, is what love is all about. This is what Jesus both showed us and did for us. Remember this when you are tempted to despair at the possibility of realizing such love. Love isn't a feeling; it's a commandment—the greatest commandment!

A recent psychological study stated "People today fall in love on the average of twenty-five times a day." The problem with this is that most people confuse their "falling in love" with love. People fall into all kinds of things, including infatuation, but this isn't love. Love goes beyond chemistry, beyond infatuation, beyond what you want and need. Love is the unreserved giving of yourself to another, for that person's benefit, in spite of how you feel. This is how God in Christ gave Himself to us.

We are free to love as Christ commanded, but there is no free love. Love is never cheap. Love is always costly. This is perhaps why so many individuals reserve love unashamedly for themselves. But this selfishness is unbiblical and sub-Christian.

How little we are able to love without Christ! I remember two friends who once gave me a simple rebuke that has remained one of the deepest criticisms I have ever received. They told me, "You don't know how to love." I was hurt, enraged, defiant, and defensive. Yet through numerous relationships I was unable to prove to my satisfaction that they were wrong. Their indictment haunted me. As I look at it now from a Christian perspective, I see that I was haunted by its truth. There was only one thing preventing me from loving: My life was Christ-less.

Without Christ all I could do was to take. Only when Christ took over my life could I love, and then only because I had first been loved. I could love because I had to love. My freedom to love came as I placed myself in submission to a holy God, a God who commands love. You see, it is all spelled out in Scripture. I don't define the parameters of my freedom. I don't decide if I want to love. I don't assess my ability to love. I love because he first loved me (1 John 4:19) and that love is sacrificial, in spite of the cost, the loss, or the danger.

I am free to go beyond the self-love that every natural (unregenerate) man finds easy. I am now free to love outside of myself. I am free to bring the model of Christ to others and forget about myself. The freedom to love (in Christ) breaks radical selfishness, which is the blight of man. The ultimate issue is love. Jesus touched all in love, regardless of the cost: "Father, forgive them, for they know not what they do" (Luke 22:34).

When we say we want love, what we mean is that we want to be loved. To be loved is passive; to love is active. By God's grace, love can go beyond such self-imposed limitations. This means those who are in Christ can love in spite of anything they say or feel.

You may be just as I was thirty years ago. I was locked into radical selfishness. If so, you need Jesus Christ. When He takes over your life, you will become free not only to love, but to change the host of life-dominating sinful patterns you thought you could never break. To these we must now turn our attention.

Study Guide

1. Consider the statement, "If one is not free in Christ, he is not free to love." Why not? What aspects of real love are impossible to achieve apart from Christ?

2. Read Ephesians 4:22–32. What aspects of the "new self" do you need to put off? What aspects do you need to put on?

3. How does expressing sacrificial love actually free you from bondage to self-love?

4. What might it look like to love someone in your life with more radical, sacrificial, Christ-like love?

10

Freedom to Change

People sometimes radically alter their lives because of great dissatisfaction with their past experience. Some become Christians but later they refuse to make lesser changes that would bring the joy and freedom they desire. The problem is, people believe that since they have taken the big step (of faith), it is now up to Christ to take the little steps for them. Christians often hate the idea that they must be the agents of change. They assume that this is unspiritual. But for God to circumvent individuals and to change them without engaging their hearts, minds and wills would make them automata.

The issue is not spiritual versus unspiritual means of change. Rather, we need to acknowledge the difficulty of change and then set out in the power of God to make needed changes. This is His plan, and it is in His Word, the Bible. Notice what He says in Ephesians 4:22–32:

> You were taught, with regard to your former way of life, to put off your old self, which is being corrupted by its

deceitful desires; to be made new in the attitude of your minds; and to put on the new self, created to be like God in true righteousness and holiness.

Therefore each of you must put off falsehood and speak truthfully to his neighbor, for we are all members of one body. "In your anger do not sin": Do not let the sun go down while you are still angry, and do not give the devil a foothold. He who has been stealing must steal no longer, but must work, doing something useful with his own hands, that he may have something to share with those in need.

Do not let any unwholesome talk come out of your mouths, but only what is helpful for building others up according to their needs, that it may benefit those who listen. And do not grieve the Holy Spirit of God, with whom you were sealed for the day of redemption. Get rid of all bitterness, rage and anger, brawling and slander, along with every form of malice. Be kind and compassionate to one another, forgiving each other, just as in Christ God forgave you.

There is no hint of passivity in this passage. It is filled with commands directed to you!

[You] put off your old self. (v. 22)
[You] be renewed. (v. 23)
[You] put on the new self. (v. 24)
[You] put off falsehood. (v. 25)
[You] (and to emphasize his target, he says, "each one of you") speak truthfully. (v. 25)

In reference to his former manner of life, that person who lived in bondage to sin is given a program by God. It is a program that involves change. The "old self" is the life of sin that previously enslaved us. After the commands in Ephesians 4 is a catalogue of sins, the essence of the old self.

We are to put off these old sinful habits by putting them to death. We have the ability to change under the Spirit's empowerment. So strong is this reality that God calls His people to put on the new self. We do not regenerate ourselves. At the same time, we do not sit back passively, waiting for sanctification to occur. God calls you to stop lying. God calls you to stop stealing. The wonderful reality is that sinners like you and I can actually stop sins that we had mastered (and had mastered us) over a lifetime of practice in service to Satan.

The great problem, though, comes not in stopping sinful habit patterns, but in replacing them with GODLY ones. This passage is also clear in that respect. Notice:

> Put off falsehood [and instead] speak truthfully. (v. 25)

> Be angry [yet] do not sin. (v. 26 NRSV)

> He who has been stealing must steal no longer, but must work, doing something useful with his own hands, that he may have something to share with those in need. (v. 28)

> Do not let any unwholesome talk come out of your mouths, but only what is helpful for building up others according to their needs. (v. 29)

> Get rid of all bitterness, rage and anger, brawling and slander, along with every form of malice. Be kind and compassionate to one another, forgiving each other, just as in Christ God forgave you. (vv. 31–32)

Change is what Jay Adams has called a two-factored process: the putting off of sin, and the putting on of righteousness.[1]

My purpose is not to describe the methodology of biblical change. This has been done well by Adams. I want to assure you that while changing your life is tough, it is much tougher to go through life mired in sin. The Scriptures teach that the way of the transgressor is hard (Prov. 13:15). It is possible to change. You have been given all you need to accomplish any change you need to make (2 Peter 1:3). In a world shouting for freedom, it is liberating to experience the victory of seeing sin smashed in your life, and exercising the freedom granted by God to forsake and flee from sin. Remember James' words: "Resist the devil, and he will flee from you" (James 4:7). Smashing sin is one aspect of resisting the devil—an enemy who wants you to fall into "all kinds of temptations" (James 1:2). It is a wonderful day when you experience what Paul said:

> No temptation has seized you except what is common to man. And God is faithful; He will not let you be tempted beyond what you can bear. But when you are tempted, He will also provide a way out so that you can stand up under it. (1 Corinthians 10:13)

So we see that change comes in the heat of our battles against Satan and under the guidance and empowerment of the Holy Spirit. In His power, we can always expect a victory . . . a victory as liberating as it is sanctifying.

Endnotes

1. Adams, J.E. *The Christian Counselor's Manual,* Presbyterian and Reformed Publishing Co., 1973, pp. 171–190.

Study Guide

1. Many Christians assume that once we have expressed faith, it's up to God to change us. What's wrong with this idea? By what means does God use us to bring about his work of change?

2. According to Ephesians 4:22–25, what is the basic two-step process of change? What five additional steps does the author outline for change?

3. Do you believe that "while changing your life is tough, it's much tougher to go through life mired in sin"? Or do you tend to think it would be easier to sin?

4. How do we obey the charge to "resist the devil, and he will flee from you" (James 4:7)? In what specific ways can we resist?

II

Freedom in Deed and Thought

*I*n the last chapter we saw that Christ frees people to live godly lives in spite of numerous difficulties and temptations. In Christ, this freedom is not only possible, but it is His standard, His command.

In this chapter, we want to go deeper. Christ frees us from sinful behavior patterns, but he also frees us from sinful thought patterns as well. This freedom doesn't come easily, but through insight, prayer, and hard work.

Christians, like most people, often find themselves paralyzed by what they think. They think they are helpless victims who must endure a barrage of distressful thoughts and thought patterns. How ridiculous! Just as we have control over what we do, so we also have control over what we think. No one and no thing (including demonic forces) can make believers think what they do not want to think. The Bible puts it even more forcefully: "Finally, brothers, whatever is true, whatever is noble, whatever is right, whatever is pure, whatever is lovely, whatever is admirable—if anything is excellent or praiseworthy—think about such things" (Phil. 4:8).

The most significant fact to notice here is that godly thinking isn't an option. You have no excuse for allowing yourself to continue sinful and self-destructive thinking.

Changing this pattern is so simple that you may be tempted to write it off as simplistic. But let me put it this way: You can't think evil if you think good. Try it. Try to think something good and something evil at the same time. Of course it is impossible. Why? Because your mind is made to hold only one thought at a time. If you hold a thought that is good, there is no room for one that is rotten. This fact is supported by one of the most basic laws of logic. The law of non-contradiction states that something cannot be both A and non-A in the same place and at the same time and in the same relationship. Your thoughts cannot be both good and evil at any given moment.

You can prove this to yourself. The very next time you are hit by a destructive or evil thought, immediately think about something righteous. It will take some concentration, but soon you will be as good at constructive thinking as you have been at destructive thinking. This is the meaning of Philippians 4:8. You are commanded to do this. "Whatever is true, whatever is noble, whatever is right, whatever is pure, whatever is lovely, whatever is admirable—if anything is excellent or praiseworthy—think about these things."

But Paul's command doesn't end on the thought level. He continues with a second command. Whatever you have learned or received or heard from me, or seen in me—put it into practice" (Phil 4:9). Thinking and doing are inextricably intertwined. It is not enough to think about what is right. You must practice it.

For example, if you realize that you have sinned against your wife, it is not enough to know that it is right to ask her forgiveness. It is necessary to go and ask her to forgive you. It is only then that the promise of Philippians 4:9 becomes operative. Then "the God of peace shall be with you".

Thinking is a major part of our lives. Wrong thinking is with each of us to some degree. But it can be smashed as a dominating force. You don't have to be ruled by a thought life that is out of control. Why? Because it's not! God by His power has put you in control. Your freedom extends into your thought life. Your freedom grants you self-control.

As a Christian you are not a slave to any sin (Rom. 6:2, 6–7). It is time to begin the battle against indwelling sin. You will see bitterness, unrighteousness, anger, envy, revenge, lust, as well as many other sinful thought patterns smashed as you submit to God and obey His commands for you.

Remember: It will take repeated practice to think rightly, but you'll get the hang of it, and soon the evil thinking that once dominated your life will disappear. You will be thinking, as Christ commanded His people, about what is "right and pure and lovely."

The next point, while it follows naturally from the points above, will probably be even more difficult to accept. But your joy and freedom in serving Christ is limitless when you appreciate it: Just as you are responsible for what you think and do, you are also responsible for what you feel.

Study Guide

1. Why is it important to change the way we think in order to change the way we act? What is the relationship between what we think and what we do?

2. Read Philippians 4:6–9. Think of a personal example for each of the "whatsoevers" in verse 8, and spend some time meditating on each.

3. Are you experiencing the "peace of God"? If not, why? What does Philippians 4:9 say is necessary to experience this peace?

4. What is the relationship between Christian freedom and self-control?

5. Read Romans 6:2–7. How does your identity as one who is no longer a "slave to sin" empower you pursue righteousness? Why do you still act like a slave sometimes?

12

Freedom and Emotion

*H*ere are some refrains I hear repeatedly in counseling:

> "He enrages me!"
> "She makes me sick!"
> "His criticisms upset me."
> "He frightens me."
> "She hurt my feelings."

We act as though other people or situations control our feelings. This is not true. People don't make us angry. Even more to the point, people can't make us angry. Situations are often provocative, but we can choose to allow ourselves to be provoked, or not. If people could actually make us angry or depressed, it would mean that we have no control over ourselves but that others do! Is that right? Do others have control over you? Most people would answer emphatically, "NO!" But they live as though they are controlled by the slightest whims of others and the host of irritating situations they face each day.

Something else must be considered. Why is it that two people respond very differently to the same stimuli? I witnessed a slight fender-bender recently in which the two participants came at each other—one with rage and fists flying, the other calm and peaceable. Why the difference? Of course there can be many reasons—genetics, experience, a fight earlier at home, what they ate for breakfast, etc.—but the fact is, the choice to be combative was open to both of them, and only one chose it.

Does this mean that only one of those two men was angry? Perhaps, but I have no way of knowing that. Both may very well have been angry, and perhaps with good cause. What is critical is not whether we feel anger or not. Anger is an emotion given by God, as all our emotions are. What is critical is how we respond when we experience anger.

The Apostle Paul is quite clear about this: "Be angry, and yet do not sin" (Eph. 4:26 NASB). What he means is simple: You are in control. You can decide whether you will allow yourself to use the angry feelings as an opportunity to sin, or as an opportunity to glorify God. There is nothing like the experience of exercising godly discipline over your feelings in a situation where previously they would seem uncontrollable.

One biblical example will help to illustrate this. Cain and Abel brought sacrifices to God. God accepted only those of Abel. Cain turned away dejected and angry. He was sullen and sulking. At this point he was confronted by God. "Why are you angry and depressed? Do well, and you will be happy again" (Gen. 4:6, 7, author's paraphrase). So true! You can spend your lifetime crying about how others cause your failures and problems and angers. What a waste of your life! How unproductive! How un-glorifying to God! How untrue! Why, then, do people behave that way? Why do people do what accomplishes nothing?

"If only my sister hadn't gotten all the attention." "Nobody loves me." Such statements allow people the ill-afforded luxury of self-pity. They are the worst cop-outs of all. People who use them don't acknowledge that they might have to love anybody. They just bemoan that they aren't loved. They'd rather whine and be miserable than risk loving others and face possible rejection, because love does involve risk.

People hate to risk because it can bring success or failure. Many people opt for never succeeding rather than risk failing. If a person never tries to succeed, at least he can say, "If I had tried, I'd have been a great success." This is where others come in. Instead of saying, "I didn't try because I chose to give in to my fear of failure (which they can never admit)," they say, "You made me fail." Few people realize that failure is just as okay as success. It's every bit as okay, as long as failure means, "I chose to try. I chose to do my best. I chose to risk. It just didn't work out." Failure is as much a part of life as success, and potentially as healthy. Why shouldn't people remain as solid in failure as in success?

People who only feel good about themselves when they're succeeding actually can't handle success any better than failure. In failure they bathe in self-pity. In success they become brash and arrogant. They are as displeasing to God either way.

People hate to fail, not because of the failure, but because they are so in love with themselves that they can't stand the thought of tarnishing the image of the lover they possess. Sadly, that image is of themselves. Yet all is not hopeless, even in regard to self-love. We will see in the next chapter how to be freed from this useless snare.

Study Guide

1. Can other people make us angry? Why or why not?

2. "What is critical is not whether we feel anger or not... but how we respond when we experience anger." How do you distinguish the feeling of anger from your response to the person or circumstance that generated that feeling?

3. What should Cain have done with his experience of anger and depression? How might the story have turned out differently?

4. Read Ephesians 4:25–27. How might these verses give you a new agenda for the next interaction in which you are tempted to respond with anger?

13

Freedom from Self-Love

Some time ago, a man I counseled described himself as "frozen." He experienced great difficulties in all his relationships. In fact he said most of them were "coming apart." As we talked, it became clear that the issue for him was not just working through the difficulties. His own diagnosis was that what he "really" needed was to be able to love himself so that he could get beyond himself.

Is that really what he needed? Most popular psychologists would say, "Yes, he is quite perceptive." He would then be fed the dogma that his maturation demands heaping portions of self-esteem and self-love. Noted Christian psychologist James Dobson says: "Whenever the keys to self-esteem are seemingly out of reach for . . . people, as in twentieth-century America, then widespread mental illness, neuroticism, hatred, alcoholism, drug abuse, violence and social disorder will certainly occur."[1]

Paul Brownbach, commenting on this quote, says, "Dobson sees a cause/effect relationship between a lack of self-acceptance and the worst personal and social problems of our times."²

This idea has been captured most eloquently by Max Sterner in "The Ego and His Own." He says, "Nothing means more to me than myself. Whether what I think and do is Christian, what do I care? Whether it is human, humane, Liberal, inhumane and illiberal, what do I care about that?"

Modern man wrongly assumes that all his personal ills would be cured if he could only love himself. He somehow comes to the conclusion that he hates himself. All around him people cry out that this is terrible. He tries gimmicks and tricks to deceive himself into self-love. After all, even many Christian counselors say, "Christ loves you so you ought to love yourself." He comes to believe these ideas, even while knowing that loving himself is really a pretty repulsive thought as well as a waste of time. Unfortunately he can't conceive of a better way and doesn't want one. He has been brainwashed to believe that the root of all bliss is enhanced self-esteem. Actually though, the quest for self (self-esteem, self-exaltation), as theologian Rousas Rushdoony points out, is what leads to depravities like Nazism. To esteem yourself is a perversion of the call to esteem others, and to love yourself is a perversion of the call to love-others. Both lead subtly to lusting for self and despising others, doing everything you can do to elevate yourself.

There is a response leveled against this teaching of self-love.³ Not only is it bad in theory; it is bad in life. It can lead to fascism on a social level, and to selfish self-centeredness on an individual level. Such selfishness, more than anything else, is what keeps man from being what God wants him to be. Man is free (at least in part) when he is free of the shackles of self-love. His eyes are off himself. As a Christian, his focus should be on Christ and others. It becomes easy to see then how the threat of failure diminishes in potency. Jesus lived and failed wretchedly by human standards, but in God's sight his "failure" was the "victory that overcame the world" (1 John 5:4). What brought this victory about? At the very least, it was the attitude, "not as I will, but as you will" (Matt. 26:39). The King of Glory relinquishes himself for the sake of others, yet we persist in clinging to self. Do we really believe Him? No! If we did, our focus would be far from ourselves. "Fix your eyes on Jesus" says the author of Hebrews (12:2). Why does this redirection liberate us? If you are glued to yourself, you are fixated on a merciless master. If, however, your love is directed to God and others, you no longer have to please yourself. The accolades that formerly defined your self-worth are no longer imperatives. You are free to love God—and He gives you room to do so, as opposed to being under the tyranny of self.

As I spoke with the "frozen" man, I suggested that it wasn't deeper self-love that he needed. I told him I wouldn't help him to love himself. I suggested that he already was so enamored with himself that all his energies had been expended in that direction. I suggested that his inner freeze was a golden opportunity to pull the walls down and allow himself to be the imperfect person he was. Then perhaps, he could rectify the numerous difficulties he had perpetrated in his relationships with others. This would occur when he looked for their needs, rather than seeking to have them meet his own. He didn't need to love himself. He needed to love them. To do this, the believer must learn to deny himself, every day. We'll see how to do this in the next chapter.

Endnotes

1. Paul Brownback, *The Danger of Self-Love*, Moody Press, Chicago, 1982, page 15.
2. Adams, J.E. *The Christian Counselor's Manual*, Presbyterian and Reformed Publishing Co., 1973, pp. 171–190.
3. Jay E. Adams, *The Christian Counselor's Manual*, Presbyterian and Reformed, 1976, pages 142, 143. Jay E. Adams, *The Biblical View of Self-Esteem, Self-Love, Self-Image*, Harvest House Publishers, 1986. Paul Vitz, *Psychology as Religion: The Cult of Self-Worship*, Eerdmans, 1977. Paul Brownback, *The Danger of Self-Love*, Moody, Chicago, 1982.

Study Guide

1. Have you ever been persuaded by this notion that self-love is necessary before we can love others? In what ways can this commitment to self-love actually enslave a person? In what ways can it even lead to harming others?

2. Many Christian counselors will say: "Christ loves you, so you ought to love yourself." What is wrong with this statement? Finish the sentence more biblically: "Christ loves you, so
   _____."

3. Read Luke 9:23. How does the life of Christ contrast with a life of self-love? How might your life of self-denial look different than a life of self-love?

14

Freedom in Denial, Cross-Bearing and Following Jesus

What I have said in the last chapter amounts to this: We must turn from self-preoccupation and its legion of selfs: self-acceptance, self-fulfillment, self-realization, self-potential, self-actualization, and self-love. I will go so far as to say that self-absorption amounts to idolatry (the chief idolatry of our culture). Freedom in a biblical sense comes only when such self-preoccupation is smashed. Notice what Jesus says: "If anyone would come after me, let him deny himself and take up his cross daily and follow me. For whoever wants to save his life will lose it, but whoever loses his life for me will save it" (Luke 9:23, 24).

The frenzy of self-seeking behavior in our society is a quest to save ourselves. Indeed the Humanist Manifesto of 1933 (and 1973) affirms, *"There is no deity to save us. We must save ourselves"* (emphasis mine). But according to Jesus, the essence of wise, soul-saving behavior begins with getting your focus off of yourself! His prescription for the ultimate blessing (salvation) comes in a threefold manner. He doesn't say that you are not to be interested in yourself but, first of all, to deny yourself. This is not moral improvement by rigorous practices. It is renouncing anything and everything that seeks priority over Jesus Christ. This is the most basic ingredient of the Christian life: the affirmation of the Lordship of Jesus Christ. The ultimate manner in which this is demonstrated is by denial of self.

Along with this affirmation of Christ's lordship is the practical outworking to "bear your cross daily." Those who confess Jesus as Lord demonstrate that confession by identifying with Jesus. They don't deny Christ in life and work, but live His commands obediently in every area of life. They often reap unpleasant consequences, for, "Indeed all who desire to live a godly life in Christ Jesus will be persecuted" (2 Tim. 3:12).

At the same time, their freedom in Christ enables them to delight in their union with Him. Their temporary afflictions are counted as trifles compared with the eternal glory He will reveal (2 Cor. 4:17–18). This does not mean that you will enjoy suffering, privation, or loss for Christ. It simply means that your relationship to Christ involves realistic assessment and choice. Difficulties come, and as a believer you can choose to be miserable or, by God's grace, to bear up and demonstrate righteousness and even nobility under all manner of affliction. You do this for the sake of Christ, as a follower of Christ, not as an unemotional ascetic. You are deeply involved with others, but your hope always remains in Christ, not other people. You do not believe that you must save yourself. On the contrary, you affirm with the apostle Peter in Acts 4:12, "Salvation is found in no one else, for there is no other name under heaven given to men by which we must be saved." This is true freedom. The pressure to try to "save yourself" is off.

The temptation to trust in yourself for salvation is one of the biggest tests in your life. Notice that even Jesus was similarly tested while He hung from the cross, atoning for our sins. The people shouted at Him, "If you are the King of the Jews, save yourself!" (Luke 23:35, author's paraphrase). He was free to burst from the bonds of nails. He was free to execute divine judgment right then and there. He was truly free, and in that freedom He dared not interfere with divine justice, even though it was upon Him. Why? Because He came not to save Himself, but us! That is why He cried out, "Father, forgive them" (Luke 23:24) .That is how He can show us the way of reconciliation—a route of denial, a path of cross bearing, and a trail of death (to self).

This is how His words and life lead us to know that the entire humanist movement is doomed, no matter how helpful and ingenious it may seem. Why? Because the Lord says that all who seek life apart from Him will ultimately lose their lives (Luke 9:24). The extent of this loss can be seen only by way of comparison. "What good is it for a man to gain the whole world, and yet lose or forfeit his very self?" (Luke 9:25). His salvation is so great that the person who might gain the whole world is still bankrupt without Him. How far our society has drifted from this is illustrated in an incident reported in a Los Angeles Times editorial, which I am repeating here in its entirety.

STUDENT SUES OVER USE OF FOUR-LETTER WORD

A Louisiana high school graduate has filed suit against school officials for censoring the valedictory speech she had planned to deliver at her commencement last spring.

The young woman, Angela Kaye Guidry, was required to submit her speech to school officials in advance. When they noted the presence of a four-letter word and language related to that word, the suit alleges, the principal refused to let her speak unless she deleted the offending language from her text.

Were these words related to a sexual practice or scatology? Were they normally heard only in locker rooms or on the football field? No, the four-letter word that offended school officials was L-O-R-D.

The lawsuit, filed by the Rutherford Institute, a Virginia-based non-profit civil liberties organization, alleges that principal Kerry Durr and school guidance counselor Sylvia Seals told Guidry she could not include the following paragraph, or anything related to this subject, in her address: "To me the most important thing in your life is not whether you have a good education or a good job, but whether or not you have the Lord in your life. It doesn't matter how many years you go to school or how successful you are in this life, if you're not doing it all for the Lord."

The suit alleges that after graduation rehearsal, Durr told her that since someone might "be offended" by the religious content of her speech, he wanted her to delete all references to her personal religious views. When she refused, Durr told her she would not be allowed to speak.

The suit also alleges that the school guidance counselor "engaged in a tirade of criticism" within earshot of Guidry's classmates and that when the student tried to walk away, the counselor "grabbed her arm and continued making derogatory and slanderous remarks" about the student's religious beliefs.

This case is especially offensive when compared to a case in Tacoma, Wash., four years ago. A high school student had delivered a speech nominating a classmate for school office. The speech was loaded with sexual innuendo. The student, Matthew Fraser, was suspended and forbidden to speak at graduation. He sued the school district and won. The case was even upheld on appeal, though the Supreme Court ultimately overturned it.

The ninth Circuit U.S. Court of Appeals, in upholding a lower court judgment against the school for abridging Fraser's First Amendment free speech rights, said, "The school district failed to establish that the student's use of sexual innuendo in the nominating speech substantially disrupted or materially interfered in any way with the educational process, and the school district violated the First Amendment when it imposed discipline on the student."

Someone should take a poll—our new method for arriving at immutable truth—and find out whether people are more offended by a student using the word L-O-R-D or using sexual innuendo. The Rutherford Institute lawyers are asking for financial damages for Angela Kaye Guidry.

But if the school is upheld in its attempt to squelch the protection of the First Amendment as it relates to speech and the free exercise of religion, it will be the Constitution that will have been seriously damaged, along with a young woman's faith in the freedoms she sees guaranteed to virtually everyone else in her country, but not to her.

Who is free? Is it the "liberated" principal and guidance counselor who "continued making derogatory and slanderous remarks" about her religious beliefs? Few individuals would call the student "free." But she is free, in the deepest sense! Not only because she refuses to serve teachers or peers, but because she is not self-serving.

"To me the most important thing in your life is not whether you have a good education or a good job, but whether or not you have the Lord in your life. It doesn't matter how many years you go to school or how successful you are in this life, if you're not doing it all for the Lord."

Snipe at it, criticize it if you will, but you can't deny it. People such as this rile their associates because they are out of step. They aren't seeking salvation by peer praise but by faith in Christ, demonstrated by obedience to Him. Why are so few like this girl? It's simple. We provide excellent role models to ensure that our children will mature into people-pleasing, God-denying Christians!

Go "out of step" and risk everything, but be sure you are in step with Christ. The prize is not only a distant salvation. It is glorious, present freedom as well. Liberated from the shackles of self-salvation, we are free to glory in His salvation, and we are free to walk as untouchable and unstoppable. This is what Paul so boldly declared: "Let no one cause me trouble, for I bear on my body the marks of Jesus" (Gal. 6:17).

This is the path of all who would come after Christ. What is truly amazing is how few take it!

Study Guide

1. Read Luke 9:23–24. What is the ultimate danger of a self-absorbed life?

2. One of the biggest temptations in life is our tendency to try and save yourself, as the Humanist Manifesto explicitly promotes. How do you fight this tendency? What is the alternative?

3. Read Luke 23:35. What was the last temptation of Christ?

4. How can a life of self-denial, cross-bearing, and even suffering be considered free? What are the benefits of such a life? What is the alternative?

15

Freedom Now

*H*ave you ever wondered why so few choose the freedom offered in Christ? Some people say, "It's not true." Others look at the messy lives, families and ministries of supposedly "Christian" people and are repulsed. Still others fear relinquishing control over their lives. All of these, and many other concerns, can be handled easily.

But there is another, more noticeable group of people who reject Christ's freedom as well. It is the vast number of Christians who live in regular defeat. Are you in that group? Does your life seem shackled to sins and habits of a lifetime? Does the cross of Christ seem unable to touch or affect your life? The problem is not in the cross! The problem is you. You need to understand how the cross can touch and penetrate your life. Do you often feel that you are living only for the second coming of Christ? Do you experience life as a slave of sin? Do you assume liberation can never come until you are taken out of the world? This chapter is for you! I want you to see that biblical freedom awaits you here and now, in and through the re-demption of Jesus Christ.

Let me give you an illustration. Following the Civil War, many black slaves, newly emancipated, returned to their former masters' plantations. Why? Was it because they loved slavery? No! They did this because they didn't know how to be free! Slav-ery was all they knew. They were told, "You're free now." This meant nothing to them. No one ever showed them how to be free. With increasing confusion and bewilderment, they often found themselves back at the master's house, doing what they knew best. They behaved like slaves, even though technically they were free.

What they needed were lessons, after generations of bondage, about how to be free. When these were not forth-coming, slavery (or its equivalent in a free society) was the path of least resistance and the lifestyle to which many returned.

So it is in the church. Many have been in bondage to nu-merous sins. For years they have struggled. They are brought to Christ and told, "Now you'll be happy," or "Now your prob-lems will be gone," or, "Now you are free." Instead they find themselves miserable, with problems that return tenfold. Free-dom in Christ seems like a lie, a delusion, a hopeless quest at best. What is the solution?

Christians need to see that while coming to Christ frees them from the consequences of sin and death in the future, it also brings them liberty now. As Paul says, "it is for freedom that Christ has set us free" (Gal. 5:1). Christians need desperately to learn how to be free when everything tries to pull them back into slavery. Freedom from sin need not be just a dream, or a hope or a vague wish. It can be reality for every Christian. This is what discipleship is all about. It is not just a future eternal life. It is a new life now.

Living free. That is what it is all about. No, I don't mean some self-serving ego trip. I don't mean Jesus as a new high. Honestly examine your life. You must notice just how much of what you say or do bears almost no resemblance to what you believe as a Christian. Everyone recognizes it. The consulting rooms of psychiatrists and psychologists are filled with people who live in chains.

New life in Christ doesn't magically produce people who say and do what they want all the time, nor should it. Biblical Christianity is meant to do something far more substantial—to produce a new life. Freedom in Christ should spur people to take the risk to live rightly before God. The goal is not to live for yourself or to seek first for yourself. But as a biblical counselor, I am always saddened at the number of people who do not live their biblically based dreams because they are fearful and anxious.

Such people live for elusive hopes way off in the future, many of which they will never enjoy (even if those hopes do materialize). They mortgage the present, the only life they have, for a future that may never come. I am not denigrating planning, providing, saving, etc. I am just saying that Jesus gives us one day to live and fight and struggle in, and He provides energies for today. "Therefore do not worry about tomorrow, for tomorrow will worry about itself. Each day has enough trouble of its own" (Matt. 6:34).

These principles were brought home to me when our family was praying about a plan to move to a farm. Everything seemed right—the time, the situation, the ministry, our lives (three small children who would love the farm)—in short, everything. At that point someone suggested we remain in the city, giving a number of reasons. My wife and I gave his concerns considerable thought and prayer. Then something hit me. If I lived according to this individual's agenda, my small children would miss the blessings of this opportunity. We would never be able to recapture that loss for them, and we shouldn't have to, since we weren't obliged to live according to someone else's plan.

We have been on Son-Flower Farm for many years now. There is one more child who was born on the farm. The children have grown up with sheep and goats, rabbits and chickens, foxes and wolves, woods and ponds, gardens and lambs. Our oldest daughter is a self-described "lamb midwife" having delivered one of our lambs that was having a very difficult birth. I've tracked wolves and foxes that harmed our flock. This may sound ideal to some, and for us it is, but it is not for everyone. The point is that we might have let it all slip by if we had made our decision based on someone else's expectations for our family.

What about you? Does this sound familiar? Many of you live like this, more than you care to admit. The choices before you may not be as big as living on a farm versus living in the city, but the daily influences that shape your life are just as significant.

I was in a northwestern city recently to speak at a rally. One evening I had a few hours off, so I asked my hosts (one of the sponsoring pastors and his wife) if they would mind if I watched a movie. Neither minded, so I invited them to join me. They said they couldn't, because they had to go to a church party. They asked me if I wanted to attend. I graciously declined. At that point they said they would really love to watch the movie with me. I said, "Let's watch it then." They both expressed regret because they "had to go" to this party, because it was expected. I then expressed my regret that they chose to live by other people's expectations. They wished they could do what they wanted, but they chose to live by the expectations of others. Why?

They thought they would have the security of keeping life in their congregation flowing smoothly because everyone was doing what was expected of them. But much of the time, it's the other way around. People despise those who give in to them and have no gumption.

We are going to have battles all along the way. We may as well be honest and live courageously. Cowardice is never a guarantee of anything but a bad conscience. This couple, after seeing my strong reaction to their decision, opened up to me. They told me about another recent situation concerning their house, which was a parsonage and thus was owned by the congregation.

This parsonage was a lovely home. More importantly, it was their home (even if they didn't own it). But the congregation was given the opportunity to buy a relatively newer house that involved less upkeep.

This family had been living in the parsonage for eleven years when they were told that the congregation was purchasing this new house, and that they'd be moved. After I probed a bit, the wife expressed bitterness and resentment, partly because her husband had kept them from really sharing their deep concern. He said he wanted to avoid hassles on anything but "big" issues. I told them that this was an area worth fighting for—partly because it was their home, and partly because it was important to his wife.

Can it ever be right to let others (over whom you have been given special oversight) make decisions for you like that? Can it be right for you? Can it be right for them? Also, if one party in the marriage feels that strongly, obviously it's not irrelevant. We often tell ourselves that these are indifferent matters, but, in reality, they eat us up. We let them consume us because we choose to deceive ourselves into taking a path that seems easier, yet is incredibly more difficult. We fail to trust Christ to see us through, regardless of the outcome. We start to compromise. Soon a good man isn't anyone's spiritual leader. He becomes the dog to kick around, until they finally kick him out. And all the while, he isn't preaching Christ; he's just saving himself, which is exactly what Jesus refused to do.

Another illustration might be helpful. Recently I received two speaking requests—one for a seminar on communication in marriage and one for a seminar on child discipline. In the hundreds of requests I have received, only once did someone tell me what the honorarium would be (sometimes there is none), and in this case, they told me the honorarium after I had already turned it down. The honorarium was very generous. I hung up and found myself regretting my decision. Then I thought, "Why don't I call up and accept it anyway?" Here is what I found myself thinking: "Rich, you're supposed to be holy. People believe that a pastor shouldn't be motivated in any way by money. If you turned it down, but now want to do it, it will appear that it is only for the dough. Further, they won't esteem you any longer." Maybe my reason for reconsidering it wasn't great, but suddenly I realized that the reason for not accepting it—pride—was worse. I knew I couldn't honor Jesus by hiding behind my pride. Besides, with an attractive remuneration, the seminar did take on a new appeal. Is that wrong? No . . . except for pastors, and other "holy" people. I called up and accepted the engagement, telling them that the proposed remuneration had changed my mind. They were thrilled and even more interested because of my honesty about it. The guilt-trip I had expected never materialized.

At the same time I was beginning to learn how to avoid guilt trips (but not guilt!). I began either asking for the honorarium or charging a fee, in suitable situations. Like most people, Christians tend to despise what comes cheap. My thinking was that I should receive a proper remuneration for work I did for people who were able to compensate me. I know that many will say, "What a materialist!" But I would see the charge of materialism as only a manipulation to work for nothing.

One can accept unfairness, however, even though it may not help people in ways they need it most. If you let yourself be treated unfairly, you mustn't let yourself become bitter. I remember a pastor recounting to me angrily about a church he spoke in, which gave him nothing afterwards for his ministry. He was still irate about it several years later. What I found amusing was that I had spoken previously in his church, and was actually scheduled to speak again (that very night) in his church. The last time I had spoken there they had failed to give me anything (including even travel expenses). I remember finding it interesting that a man who was so concerned for his own fair treatment hadn't been concerned about the appropriate treatment of someone else in that same situation.

The well-known preacher John MacArthur tells an amusing account of being asked to preach in a nearby church and refusing the invitation. Immediately they said, "We wanted to give you $5,000 for this speaking engagement." Even someone of the stature of John MacArthur was disturbed by that turn of events. I was impressed that he could even talk about it! Pastors, holy men of God, are people too. We all struggle with these things. It is vital to work them out so that they don't work themselves out in bitterness, greed or envy. My solution is simply (in appropriate situations) to say what I believe is fair. Sure, some do not care for that. That is their decision. I mustn't let it influence me in my attitude towards them. Inevitably there will be consequences for any decision we make. Being aware of this, we can make decisions that maximize our usefulness to God and our freedom in Christ in serving Him. Often non-confrontation is not the loving way out or the best way out, but only the easiest way out. We should be careful not to confuse them. But how confusing things can become.

Everything becomes dichotomized, like Christian (spiritual) services versus worldly (secular) services. The services of a psychiatrist or psychologist cost $150 an hour, yet a completely competent pastor or biblical counselor is viewed as being worth nothing! I would never want to place a price tag on the gospel, but many in the ministry bear the responsibility for a gospel that is cheap and irrelevant in the eyes of the church, let alone the world.

Many in the ministry view themselves as irrelevant, especially alongside professionals with impressive degrees. Somewhere along the way, Christ's men must stand up and take risks, regardless of the church, the world, friends, or enemies. What is at stake is more than the credibility of the individual. It is the credibility of the gospel. As we take an honest stand for what is true, or right, or biblical, or important to us, we will experience the freedom Christ offers. This doesn't mean we will be successful. It doesn't mean we will win our cause. But whether we win or lose, in Christ, we win. This is what biblical freedom is all about.

Study Guide

1. Are you living in regular defeat, shackled to the sins and habits of your past? Why? Which of your reasons for living

this way are outside of yourself? Which are within you? What are some of the resources in Christ of which you are not taking hold?

2. Name two or three of the temptations that draw you back toward a life of slavery. Why are they so powerful? In what ways are they ultimately empty?

3. Read Matt 6:25–34. What are some of the ways that you worry excessively about tomorrow? Which of God's provisions for your needs now might you be missing?

4. What kinds of compromises can result from letting others make decisions for you? How might these compromises damage both your own freedom in Christ, and your relationships?

16

Freedom to Serve God Rather Than Self

*D*oes it sound like I'm telling you how to "be your own best friend,", or how to "take care of number one?" Am I suggesting that you simply do what you want in order to avoid being manipulated by others? No! I'm not at all trying to facilitate Christian self-seeking. In fact, as I have written earlier, I'm strongly opposed to it, because the Bible is strongly opposed to it.

The goal of life is to glorify God, and the means by which one does that is through a holy life. We are not to satisfy cravings, lusts, passions, and appetites. There is a fine line between allowing yourself to be guilt-manipulated (by others' expectations) and refusing to be manipulated for selfish reasons. This fine line is the Word of God, which points to the ultimate reality: God Himself. We serve Him. He is the One who reveals in His Word how we should live. Christians often pay only lip service to this. They are motivated by feelings instead of revelation.

For example, that pastor acted as though it was a dictate of revelation to "not let an issue (the house) cause trouble." Now I know we can find Scripture to support for not dealing with the issue. For example, "If it is possible, as far as it depends on you, live at peace with everyone" (Rom. 12:18) could be used. Verses such as "Let not a root of bitterness in your midst cause trouble" (Heb. 12:15) might be used to support a confrontational stance. But simple proof-texting can be used to support almost anything. How then should we proceed? We need biblical principles to guide us where texts are claimed for both sides of an issue. This is what I meant earlier. One pastor might have no trouble accepting the housing limitations imposed by the congregation. Another might. Should this pastor have done what he did? Or should he have opposed his congregation?

Were there biblical principles to show him a better course of action in an otherwise neutral situation? Yes. The principle here is incredibly simple! Whatever the Bible commands we must do, and whatever the Bible prohibits we must not do! In situations in which the Bible neither commands nor prohibits, we have liberty. Now, the Bible does not command pastors to go to church parties. The Bible also does not prohibit them from going. This makes things difficult. Christians often like clearer directives. Non-Christians often deride Christians for this tendency; "You think you have all the answers!" They are wrong. Most decisions fall into that gray area (from our perspective—not from God's) leaving us many options and difficult decisions. My point is, just because you do things that others expect you to do, doesn't mean that you're serving God. It is not even good to say, "I know I am doing this because others want me to." Am I suggesting that an individual isn't free to live that way (according to others' expectations) in the numerous "neutral" situations? Yes! You are not free to live that way. You are free only to serve God, which means that a situation itself may he neutral, but our choices are never neutral. Paul says of true Jews (believers), "their praise is from God and not from men" (Rom. 2:29).

Christians must move beyond living in ways that can easily

lead to defensiveness, bitterness and animosity. Of course, no situation invariably leads to bitterness or animosity just because someone accedes to the desires of others. We must make certain that we don't blame our decision on others. We must also not dwell on it and thus allow potential resentment. Most importantly, we must have something in mind that allows us to choose in this fashion. (It is unbiblical to believe these "self-sacrificing" choices to be pious.)

Serving God often means disappointing the expectations of others, sometimes our loved ones and best friends. Yet it is important in helping you to become your own person before a holy God. You must always strive to meet His expectations, refusing to take the way of least possible resistance. At the same time, we must be careful not to live as Christians who invariably claim "Christian liberty" out of lack of concern for others. Thus the believer lives with a particular tension that only the Word of God has the wisdom to resolve. It is to this resolution we now direct our attention.

Study Guide

1. How does Scripture help you distinguish between the two extremes of allowing yourself to be guilt-manipulated versus being self-seeking?

2. Think of some clear Biblical commands about what we must do. Now think of some areas of life—particularly church events—that the Bible does not command us to do. Do you understand the liberty you have in these areas? Are you able to distinguish between serving God and serving men?

3. Read Romans 2:29. Whose praise matters most? What does it look like to seek his praise rather than the praise of men?

17

Freedom from Demanding Our Own Rights

*L*et's look at three categories of life relating to freedom. First of all, there are things God commands us to do, such as "loving God with all our heart, soul, mind, and strength." Secondly, there are things God prohibits us from doing, such as "Thou shall not murder." The third area involves the mass of things in our life about which God does not directly speak in the Scriptures. These are known as "things indifferent" or things in which Christians have liberty (either to do or not to do). Much has been made of this liberty, to the point that that it often becomes a license to sin.

Christians commonly say, "I have Christian liberty" to do this or that, or they say, "No one can show me that such and such is wrong" in order to justify downright selfishness. On the surface, they may be correct. At the same time, the believer's real liberty goes far beyond being able to do all kinds of things, even things that weaker brothers (1 Cor. 8:7) can't do in good conscience. While it is true that we must not do what we do because others expect us to (1 Cor. 10:29), our liberty is not to proceed arrogantly on the basis of so-called "Christian liberty," or worse, because we consider ourselves the "stronger brother." How then should we proceed? Paul's explanation in 1 Corinthians 8 separates the mature believer from the immature believer, even as it goes beyond distinctions of strong or weak (1 Cor. 8:7), free or bound (1 Cor. 8:9), to ethical maturity and biblical freedom.

In Corinth there were many idols. Before their conversion to Christianity, the Corinthians served these idols and devoted themselves to them. Part of this service included the sacrifice of meats to their so-called gods. Of course idols cannot eat, but priests can. What the priests were unable to eat was sold in the market. Along came the Apostle Paul with the gospel of Jesus Christ into this idolatrous culture. Many were converted. Many of those converted were from the same heathen groups that had formerly devoted themselves to idols and participated in all kinds of sacrifices. So far, so good.

Then a problem emerged. Some who were converted realized how slavish and foolish their devotion to idols had been. If they were in a situation in which meat was served which only an hour ago had been offered to idols, they would eat without any qualm. After all, they could say, "We know there is no such thing as an idol in the world" (1 Cor. 8:4). On the other hand, their brethren, converted from the same idolatry, remembered how deeply idolatry had once gripped their lives. They could not imagine eating meat that had ever been connected in any way with idolatry. To them it was idol worship.

Problems arose between the two groups. They sent a letter to Paul asking about this issue and several others. The stronger brethren who could eat anything knew assumed that Paul would defend their position; it made sense! After all, as they saw it, their liberty was at stake. Speaking then to the issue of liberty (not meat), did Paul encourage it?

Paul makes it clear that these stronger brethren speak according to knowledge (1 Cor. 8:1). Even so, he declares immediately that knowledge without love is only arrogance (vv.

1–3). Yes, there is no such thing as an idol (v. 4), but this was not the only issue. There is liberty here, but what is liberty without love? From a heavenly perspective, "we are neither the worse, if we do not eat, nor the better if we do eat" (1 Cor. 8:8). What must motivate us is neither knowledge nor liberty, but love (v. 1). How then does love motivate us? Paul answers: "Therefore, if what I eat causes my brother to fall into sin, I will never eat meat again, so that I will not cause him to fall" (v. 13).

This answer takes us to the essence of Christian love, liberty and maturity. It points to a principle: for the sake of his brothers, things he is completely free to do he will never do again, if it causes them to sin. He will choose to relinquish his rights for the sake of Christ. The essence of holiness here is not giving up sins, but giving up rights. Holiness, you see, is being like the Holy One who called you (1 Peter 1:15). The Holy One who called us never "gave up" sin; He was without sin! Rather, he gave up His rights and prerogatives for the sake of His bride. Now we are called to do the same when the welfare of our brothers and sisters is at stake. This is not living according to their expectations or standards. It is a renunciation of our rights when the assertion of those rights may bring ethical harm to another. Freedom in Christ is never as simple and clear-cut as we might like to think.

The willing relinquishment of biblical rights is a difficult choice for Christians to make, especially when, upon conversion, we lost our perceived "right" to sin. There are going to be times when we will be forced to decline our rights. We should be prepared to do so. Furthermore, in an age of selfishness and self-centeredness, this corrective action is essential in demonstrating precisely that the love of Christ is not seeking one's own pleasure or benefit, but that of others.

In 1 Corinthians 8, it seems like all the force comes down against those who exercise their liberty in areas that potentially harm weaker brothers. Romans 14 balances the picture, warning both both parties. The strong must not despise or hold in contempt the weak, and the weak must not judge the strong (v.

3). Even as the strong relinquish their rights, the weak must not legislate for the church. The strong must remain strong. The weak must grow strong. Meanwhile, the strong must not force the weak to be like them, and the weak must not force the strong to give up their strength. Again, biblical love is the answer, providing acceptance for both strength and weakness in the body.

I once was interviewed by a Christian newspaper in the Netherlands. The interviewers and others present were guzzling strong, black coffee. They poured some for me and were a bit surprised when I refused. They were all smoking cigarettes or pipes. They asked me if I smoked. I replied, "No." They looked at me and said, "Don't you believe in Christian liberty?" I looked at them and said, "Don't I have the liberty to not do those things?"

It is so easy to be inconsiderate of our brother's point of view, and unloving in judging his motives. We may have much knowledge, but without love it is arrogant, proud, and boastful. A Christian is not free to be like this, no matter how right he is. Love relinquishes even rights, that Christ may be glorified in the Church.

With this as a backdrop, let us now move to another surprising twist in the issue of Christian liberty.

Study Guide

1. Christians have liberty in those areas where the Bible is silent. But what are the limits of this liberty?

2. Read 1 Corinthians 8:1–13. Paul distinguishes here between "weak," and strong, or mature, believers. How can you strive to become mature in exercising your liberty without trampling weaker believers?

3. If the essence of holiness is not giving up sins, but giving up "rights," what rights might God be calling you to give up for his sake and the sake of others?

4. Think of a contemporary situation in which a strong believer and a weak believer might come into conflict. Now read Romans 14:1–23. Rephrase Paul's instruction to each person in your own words.

18

Freedom from Holiness

*O*f all the liberties the Christian enjoys, there is one that is most relevant to our present endeavor. The Christian is first and foremost free from holiness. You may wonder how I can say that. After all, the Scriptures constantly demand holiness—consider one such passage: "But just as He who called you is holy, so be holy in all you do; for it is written: 'Be holy, because I am holy'" (1 Peter 1:15,16, quoting Lev. 19:2). How then can I say that we are free from holiness?

We need to understand holiness according to the Bible and not our own perception. Holiness is moral perfection. It is purity. It is separateness from sin and from evil of any kind. By nature, man cannot please God with attempts at holiness. Isaiah 64:6 declares, "All our righteous acts are like filthy rags." Paul affirms this indictment tenfold in Romans 3:10–18:

> As it is written, "There is no one righteous, not even one; there is no one who understands, no one who seeks God. All have turned away, they have together be-

come worthless; there is none who does good, not even one." "Their throats are open graves; their tongues practice deceit." "The poison of vipers is on their lips." "Their mouths are full of cursing and bitterness." "Their feet are swift to shed blood; ruin and misery mark their ways, and the way of peace they do not know." "There is no fear of God before their eyes."

Am I suggesting that the Christian is "free from holiness" because he has none? Is God cruelly taunting us when He says, "Be holy, because I am holy"? Is God a liar and His Word untrue?

Of course not. God never taunts His people or expects them to do the impossible. The answer is that God Himself has done the impossible for us: "With God all things are possible" (Matt. 19:26). You see, without faith in Christ, "it is impossible to please God" (Heb. 11:6). Without holiness, no one can stand in God's presence (Heb. 12:14). The resolution is simple: "God made Him who had no sin to become sin for us, so that in Him we might become the righteousness of God" (2 Cor. 5:21). Our boast is never in our righteousness, but His. Romans 3:25–26 reminds us that God in Christ "passed over the sins previously committed" in order to demonstrate "His righteousness at the present time, so that He would be just and the justifier of the one who has faith in Jesus."

This gives the believer what the Reformers called an "alien righteousness." That is, believers possess a righteousness not of themselves, but "through faith in Jesus Christ" (Rom. 3:22). Are believers holy? Do they fulfill the repeated commands to be holy? No and yes.

No, because the holiness of believers is never something in and of themselves. It is "through faith." It is not my righteousness. Whatever I am or have done, no matter how noble or worthy it may appear to either me or the world; it is bereft of any saving merit in the sight of God. In that sense then, in God's sight believers are not holy.

Conversely, believers are holy in a deeper, more profound and more significant sense. Jesus bore our sin in His death, so He declares us to be without sin in his sight. In the same way, we bear His righteousness and are declared righteous. This is the "alien righteousness" in which the Reformers gloried. Their glory was Christ's righteousness and thus, because of Him, they could be what they knew to be impossible for them: holy. Christ is not only the basis of our justification (as the One who declares us not guilty), but also the basis of our actual holiness. Paul says that Christ, "has become for us wisdom from God—that is, our righteousness, holiness, and redemption" (1 Cor. 1:30).

But even though Christ's righteousness is imputed to us, it doesn't make us inwardly righteous, or holy, or even make us "feel" holy. It simply makes us holy! This means that we are treated by God as though we are holy. This gives every believer the full pardon of all his sins and guilt and a full and just claim to eternal life.

With this truth in view, we return to our opening point. We are "free from holiness." Now we can understand the liberty in view. Apart from Christ, the demands of holiness can only crush and kill us. What despair! As Paul cries, "Wretched man that I am! Who will rescue me from this body of death?" (Rom. 7:24). Nothing can deliver us from this death—nothing, that is, except Christ. What then does his deliverance mean? It means we no longer grope after a holiness that is impossible to achieve. It means that Christ has set us free from the clutches of an angry God whose judgment falls eternally upon all who have not received His holiness by faith. More positively, it means that we can be all that He intends us to be, in some ways without being anything at all!

The Christian is the freest person in the world. No, he can't do whatever he wants, but what a banal definition of freedom that is! Surprisingly, the Christian is free most precisely because he doesn't have to attain (by his own efforts) his own righteousness.

What freedom is there in sin? Those who say God is dead

act as if all is permitted, and the result is AIDS or Chlamydia or Herpes. Three cheers for freedom! But for the Christian, everything true is permitted. "All things are lawful for me" (1 Cor. 6:12), declares Paul. He means, "all things lawful." In Christ he is a son of the Law. He is now free from the slavish servitude to legalism that marked his career as a Pharisee. In all of this, we can see Paul's development in his faith. He is both obedient and free at the same time.

> But whatever was to my profit I now consider loss for the sake of Christ. What is more, I consider everything a loss compared to the surpassing greatness of knowing Christ Jesus my Lord, for whose sake I have lost all things. I consider them rubbish, that I may gain Christ and be found in Him, not having a righteousness of my own that comes from the law, but that which is through faith in Christ—the righteousness that comes from God and is by faith. (Phil. 3:7–9)

This is Paul's legacy for the church. Our freedom is in the righteousness that comes from God—not ourselves. What freedom! Every individual (even the most hardened perverts, reprobates and murderers) defines his life by some form of righteousness. Many people think they are Christians because they are "good." But the Christian is through with such stuff. We don't boast in our badness, but we know "no one is good"! Our hope begins and ends in the Lamb. This takes all the pressures off us. He has done it! He has redeemed us; He has made us righteous. As Paul says, "He who began a good work in you will carry it on to completion until the day of Christ Jesus" (Phil. 1:6). With such promises, how can you be downcast? When you see things as they are, you realize that in Christ's righteousness you are truly the most free of all people. You are free from any legalistic notion of holiness that deadens and kills. Now you awaken to the new reality that you are free for holiness. You are freed to be all He wants you to be.

Study Guide

1. Read Romans 3:10–18. What is the difference between our perception of holiness and the biblical standard of holiness?

2. If the Bible calls us to holiness, how can we say we are "free from holiness"?

3. If you understand yourself as having an "alien righteousness"—the righteousness of Christ—how should that affect your relationships with non-Christians? How should it affect your relationships with Christians?

4. Re-read Philippians 3:7–9. Name some things in your own life that were "to your profit" that you "now consider loss compared to the surpassing greatness of knowing Christ Jesus"?

19

Freedom for Holiness

*T*he Christian should delight in his freedom. Of all people, his joy should be greatest. He has been delivered from the demands of an absolutely holy God who requires absolute holiness; a demand no human being except Christ could ever fulfill. Christ has been made our holiness (1 Cor. 1:30). We have become righteous by faith (Rom. 3:22). Does this excuse us from living righteously? Roman Catholicism has said that the idea that anyone could be declared judicially righteous without his own moral effort would produce immorality. They called such declarative justification a "legal fiction."

Does imputation lead to immorality? Paul's response is unequivocal: "By no means! We died to sin; how can we live in it any longer?" (Rom. 6:1, 2). Paul says that we are to renounce lives of sin because we have "died to sin"! That is, Christ died to sin, and as we participate in that death through faith, we, too, have made a definitive break with sin. Is there a danger of immorality? No more than placing a "morality trip" on people prevents immorality! The believer is freed from the snare of sin because he is "dead to sin" (Rom. 6:2, 7, 8, 11). Yet that description is just half of the truth. We are also "alive to God in Christ Jesus" (Rom. 6:11). What does this new life mean?

It means holy or moral living, an upright life. I am not speaking at this point of the judicial righteousness imputed to us, but a righteousness that develops as part of the sanctifying process in us. There is no contradiction in what I have been saying! We are free from pursuing holiness for our salvation. At the same time, we are now free for a life of holiness. Freedom to live righteously is our new freedom. Before we became Christians, we thought we were free, but we were not. Paul says that we were "slaves of sin, which leads to death" (Rom. 6:16). He goes on to state: "When you were slaves of sin, you were free from the control of righteousness" (Rom. 6:20). There is a somber note near the end of that sixth chapter. It concerns the terrible consequence of our bondage to sin: "for the wages of sin is death" (Rom. 6:23).

People without Christ delude themselves. They think they are free. They do have uncoerced choice, but their sinful nature only leaves them free to sin. Freedom to sin, freedom to die, freedom to end up in hell— is that a freedom worth having?

Many Christians feel bound, even though they should feel free. The freedom given by Christ is not active in their lives. Yet in spite of how they feel, Paul says they are free; they "have been set free from sin" (Rom. 6:22). That's right. Formerly we were slaves of sin, perhaps while ranting about our freedom. Now we are free, perhaps while feeling bound. How do we practice freedom and feel free?

Paul continues: "But now that you have been set free from sin and have become slaves to God, the benefit you reap leads to holiness" (Rom. 6:22). The same idea is found earlier in the chapter as well. "For just as you used to offer the parts of your body in slavery to impurity and ever-increasing wickedness, so now offer them in slavery to righteousness leading to holiness" (Rom. 6:19).

The point is simple and unmistakable. We are a holy people (1 Peter 2:9). We are marked by a holy and righteous life. Accordingly, we conduct ourselves as those in the bonds of righteousness. Just as we were once committed to sin and wholeheartedly gave ourselves over to it, now we are to be wholeheartedly committed to the pursuit of holiness. This is the beauty of holiness.

The popular psychologies of our age all attempt to correct the frustrations and disappointments and despairs of life. Most have a gimmick which, when religiously applied, promises nirvana. Almost all, including the many Christian how-to approaches, avoid the one solution that can result in true holiness and freedom. They fail to mention the only standard or measure of true holiness: God's Law.

God's revealed Law is the only standard for practicing holiness. I am not saying that holiness for justification is attained by law-keeping, nor is holiness for sanctification achieved primarily by our own efforts. We cooperate in our sanctification, but it is by the grace of God and the work of the Holy Spirit in us. The goal of the Spirit's work and our cooperation is obedience to God's Law. David found God's Law a delight (Psalm 119). All believers should delight in God's Law, but many do not. Why?

Study Guide

1. If Christians are free from pursuing our own holiness for salvation, then what is our motivation for pursuing holiness for sanctification?

2. Can you be "dead to sin" even if you feel very much alive to it? How do you understand and combat indwelling sin?

3. How do you practice the freedom of being "alive to righteousness"?

4. What is the Christian's standard of holiness?

20

Freedom and Law

As a young Christian, I accepted an idea that I didn't really understand. I also fought it. The idea was that I had to obey God's Law. I knew the Scriptures taught that David both loved and delighted in God's Law. I knew I should obey God's Law, but I never believed I could love or delight in it. God's Law seemed to deprive me of all kinds of fun. I know many Christians feel that way. What I didn't see then was that God wasn't robbing me of joys, but rather providing me with real joys. He wasn't stealing my freedom to enjoy life, but educating me to enjoy the best and fullest life. When Jesus came, He declared, "I have come that you would have life, and have it to the full" (John 10:10).

Christians often forget that God's Law is an instrument of His goodness to His creatures. He made us. He knows where life and happiness may be found, and His Law directs us to it. When we choose to follow His Law, we choose goodness and joy. Our choice honors God, but it also serves our best interest. Thank God that Christ has freed us to choose His Law.

I remember a man I counseled who looked me right in the

eye and declared that he planned to continue his homosexual behavior. Furthermore, he claimed that this was in accordance with the words of Paul. Disregarding what Paul has written directly against homosexuality (Rom. 1:27–28; 1 Cor. 6:9-11; 1 Tim. 1:10), this man told me that Paul said "everything is permissible for me" (1 Cor. 6:12). What is most amazing about his use of that verse is that it immediately follows one of Paul's explicit condemnations of homosexuality! Is Paul saying that the behavior he condemned is lawful? Of course not! He is simply saying that while all lawful things are lawful for him, he won't even do all that he is allowed to do, because he has come to see that "not everything is beneficial" (1 Cor. 6:12).

By nature we hate the Law of God. Look at the extent we go to avoid it. We set up our own standards instead of God's. We believe we will be more free if we kick over even the traces of God's Law. We don't want to be ordered around by anyone, and we develop intricate theological systems to keep us from such subservience—even though God's standard is perfect.

Once while I was teaching a Bible study, a man who attended it said he had been taught that the Law was "garbage." He noted a book called "Satan is Alive and Well on Planet Earth," by the best-selling author Hal Lindsey. In this book Lindsay says, "The Law just doesn't speak to us any more as a basis of operation in the Christian life." Even leading evangelicals such as Lindsey seem to hate the thought of God's Law as an authoritative standard for us today.

I am increasingly convinced that one of the main reasons for the mass of confusion I confront in my counseling practice is the false teaching coming from Christian pulpits on this issue of the place of the Law of God in the believer's life. Without the Law, there are no standards. Each new situation must uncover its own norms. This may sound like freedom, but it is a freedom that men and women cannot handle. God did not design us for this kind of freedom. As a result, we become enslaved to confusion, indecision, paralysis, and despair.

A young man once came to me asking for help. He said that

he was the leader of a church singles group with over 200 members and was doing a great deal of counseling. Now a problem had surfaced in his life. He had become involved with a young woman in the group, and the physical attraction had grown. They were in danger of serious sexual sin. When they went to their pastor for help, his counsel was, "Have you thought about mutual masturbation?" Is this God's Law of sexual purity? Has the church lost all recognition of God's standard?

What do you think I told him? Should I agree that since they had not directly united their sexual organs, this was a fine resolution? Or should I point out that mutual masturbation was a form of sexual intercourse? Surely that pastor's counsel was in conflict with Paul when he said, "Treat . . . younger women as sisters—with absolute purity " (1 Tim. 5:2).

I asked him, "Is that how you would treat your sister?" Then I quoted Paul's words, "It is better to marry than to burn with passion" and told him that his choice could not be mutual masturbation and sexual pleasure without marriage. Those were the only choices he had: marriage or burning (which meant for him the inevitable sexual frustration).

Perhaps you think I am too simplistic for the twentieth century. But if we reject Paul's inspired simplicity for a "broader" interpretation, what have we done but condone adultery, homosexuality—and by implication, homosexual marriage and ordination to minister in the church as well. Such churches have no connection with the Church of the Living God.

How can we have life-giving freedom? We gain it by coming to a knowledge of our sin, renouncing it, and walking according to the standards in the Bible. In Romans 7 we read, "I would not have known about coveting if the law had not said, 'You shall not covet'" (v. 7). What an instructive statement! Knowledge of our sin comes through the Law! Not only is the Law our standard for defining righteousness; it is our standard for defining sin. John says, "Sin is lawlessness" (1 John 3:4).

Paul understood his sinful lawlessness in the light of the commandments. Only then did he cry, "Wretched man that I am!"

and looked for a Savior: "Who will set me free from this body of death?" (Rom. 7:24). The Law was not his liberator, but his accuser, and Paul knows it. "Thanks be to God—through Jesus Christ our Lord" (Rom. 7:25). He moves immediately to one of the fundamental truths of the Gospel: "Therefore, there is now no condemnation for those who are in Christ Jesus" (Rom. 8:1). This is his conclusion. The Law, our standard, can not free us because we cannot keep it. Thus it condemns us, as it reveals our sin. But Christ, our righteousness, could and did free us. This is the basis of true liberty. We are freed to walk in and delight in a holy Law which previously was our condemnation.

But let us remember that we walk in submission to God and under the rule of His King and Commander, Jesus Christ. This relationship is hard for any unregenerate mind to fathom, but until we grasp it, the full implications of our freedom will be hidden from us.

Every commander of any stature imposes rules on his subjects. You can call them principles, demands, or anything you like, but he invariably legislates in the areas over which he exerts control. Thus, your boss at work has rules for you to follow in the workplace, but has no say over your life after hours. No (modern) ruler has ever asked for (let alone received) absolute control of his subjects in every area of their lives.

Yet Jesus is not a modern commander; He is history's exception. As the Lord of heaven and earth, Jesus exerts absolute authority over every area of life. What is more, He declares that His rules provide the only route to freedom: "If the Son sets you free, you will be free indeed!" (John 8:36).

Given this fact, what kind of comprehensive law system could He possibly enjoin upon us, which would still allow us to be free? The answer is the Law of God—the very system that many say doesn't speak to us any more. It is the most misused, misunderstood system of law in the world today. In fact, although it comes directly from God, there is not one nation on earth that employs it. Even some Christians say that the Law of God is not meant for them today. Is this so? Let us see.

I spoke of our Bible study visitor who was taught in a Bible believing, evangelical church that "the Law is just so much garbage!" Could he have heard correctly? Could any Christian view God's Law that way? Sadly, they often do.

Christians are being taught a system of belief that separates law from Christian living. They are taught that life in Christ has everything to do with grace and nothing to do with law. They are being taught that the Law was in force only until Christ. Where do these teachers get this? It certainly does not come from the Bible. Where, then?

There are numerous sources. Many of the most popular evangelical leaders teach it. Hal Lindsay says in the same book, "It is imperative that we realize that Law and Grace are complete systems in themselves . . . they are mutually exclusive." He goes on to say that "the tyrannical, perfectionist husband is the Law of God. In the broader sense [the Law] also represents the sin nature . . . and Satan himself."

With misunderstandings such as these, is it any wonder that the Law is disregarded? How many people want to be wedded to a "tyrannical, perfectionist husband"? Lindsay makes it appear that anyone who follows the Law is in for a life of subjection to tyranny.

If there ever was anyone who had tried to live and be justified by the Law, it was Paul. He put it this way: "As to the righteousness which is in the Law, [I was] found blameless" (Phil. 3:6 NASB). Paul never found peace with God, freedom from guilt, or freedom from sin through his law-keeping efforts. He was a murderer, persecuting the church (Phil. 3:6). His deliverance dawned only when he saw that his best efforts were no better than "filthy rags" (Isa. 64:6), and when he claimed the righteousness of Christ. His efforts had been sincere, strenuous, and in some ways excellent, but they had not saved him from his guilty knowledge of lawbreaking and condemnation on that basis.

Paul was trying to placate the holy God of heaven with his own good works. He was trying to justify himself. This was futile because he was in bondage to sin. When God saved Paul, everything changed. His understanding of the purpose and use of the Law were changed. If he viewed keeping the Law as a way to free him from guilt, he would remain guilty forever. Suddenly, a new view of the Law emerged. He came to see that the Law, while it couldn't justify, still functioned as a standard by which to gauge his own integrity, and a standard for regenerate life.

Paul had a new relationship to the Law. He let the Law convict him of sin, while exulting in his freedom from law-keeping as a way to avoid condemnation. For Christ's sake, he was now regarded by God as a law keeper rather than a law breaker. He also had a new attitude towards the Law. "I joyfully concur with the Law of God in the inner man" (Rom. 7:22 NSAB). Paul knew that the standard of God's Law was right, and now that he had been delivered from its condemnation he could enter into a life of joyful obedience. This obedience couldn't save him, but it would deepen the freedom from the tyranny of sin to which he had been called.

He agreed with the prophets. David said, "O how I love Thy law. It is my study all the day" (Psa. 119:97 KJV). Isaiah wrote, "The Lord was pleased for his righteousness' sake to make the law great and glorious" (42:21 NASB). Jesus said, "I have not come to abolish the law but to fulfill it." Eventually Paul would say that the Law is "holy" and "spiritual" (Rom. 7:12, 14).

While the Old Testament was an age of grace, now we are in an age of fuller revelation of God's saving grace. The way of grace is no longer obscure, but fully revealed in the work of Christ. The change from Old to New Testaments did not bring a change in how we are saved. Man has always been saved by grace through faith (Gen. 15:6). While the law had always demanded obedience from our hearts (Deut. 10:16; Jer. 4:4), now there is no excuse. As Jesus put it, "Unless your righteousness surpasses that of the scribes and Pharisees, you will not enter the kingdom of heaven" (Matt. 5:20). The low standard of the Pharisees could not be the standard of the people. Jesus explained how the Pharisees prided themselves on their external observance of God's Law, while neglecting his true standard of heart-obedience to his Law.

> You have heard that it was said to people long ago, "Do not murder, and anyone who murders will be subject to judgment." But I tell you that anyone who is angry with his brother will be subject to judgment. Again, anyone who says to his brother, "Raca," is answerable to the Sanhedrin. But anyone who says, "you fool!" will be in danger of the fire of hell. (Matt. 5:21–22)

> You have heard that it was said, "Do not commit adultery." But I tell you that anyone who looks at a woman lustfully has already committed adultery with her in his heart. (Matt. 5: 27–28)

Christ set an even higher standard than the externalistic obedience demanded by the Pharisees. Freedom in Christ is not a legalistic or slavish observance of law. That is bondage and condemnation. Nor is freedom in Christ rejecting God's Law. This is antinomianism (literally "against the Law"). Freedom in Christ consists of two separate concepts which always function together. One is freedom from condemnation because Christ has graciously paid the penalty for sin (justification). The other freedom is the freedom to begin to keep God's Law both inwardly and outwardly, because we are released from slavery to our sinful nature (regeneration and sanctification).

In this context we can understand the freedom we have in our new life in Christ. Read on!

Study Guide

1. Have you ever found yourself accepting a low view of God's Law? Why do you think it's so appealing to believe that God's Law is no longer relevant to us?

2. What does "all things are lawful for me" (1 Cor. 6:12) mean? Does "all things" mean any thing?

3. How does the Law of God help us obtain life-giving freedom? At what point is the Law alone unable to give us that freedom?

4. After we have acknowledged our sin, what should we do next?

5. Consider that the Law of God was given to us by the same merciful, gracious, loving creator who sent his Son to die in our place. How does this fact affect your view of the Law?

6. What is the difference between the grace revealed in the Old Testament and the grace revealed in the New Testament?

21

Freedom And The New Life

*T*he new life of a believer in Jesus Christ is not some theoretical principle. It is a present, actual reality. It is the day-by-day experience of "new mercies" (Lam. 3:22–23). Nor is it a sad, frustrated existence. We daily expect and experience the merciful visitation of our gracious Father in heaven, enabling us to act with courage for him!

By contrast, most people are gripped by fears of one kind or another. The greatest of these fears is the fear of death. The book of Hebrews states that all human beings are "held in slavery by their fear of death" (Heb. 2:15). The new life in Christ delivers us from this bondage. We have "died to sin" (Rom. 6:2). As those who are "alive from the dead" (Rom. 6:13 NASB), we know our life is changed. We cannot and must not "continue in sin" (Rom. 6:1 NASB). The new life, in making us new beings, leaves us as slaves of God.

Peter shows us what it means to have a new life in Christ. "His divine power has [already] granted to us everything pertaining to life and godliness" (2 Peter 1:3 NASB). This is a revolutionary idea. Understand it. You already have everything necessary to live a godly life. Of course, this means you also have complete responsibility for your life and actions. There are no excuses. The devil didn't make you do it. I don't mean to suggest that the new life is merely "responsibility," but the emphasis in evangelical teaching has been so focused on escape from future hell that it is imperative to point out that the new life isn't only escape from death and hell. It is also the conquest of sin now, even as we wait for the perfection of heaven. It is the practice of holiness, obedience and righteousness now!

Peter notes that the new life involves diligence, faith, moral excellence, knowledge, self-control, perseverance, godliness, and brotherly love. Each of these Christian virtues is demanded by God's Law and to be sought by believers as attainable and enjoyable.

Many people turn to Christianity hoping that sins and struggles will be taken from them, and that they won't have to battle any longer. However, escape from corruption as described in the Word requires effort. 2 Peter 1:5 (NASB) says that you should be "applying all diligence"—that is, to devote yourselves wholly to growth in godliness. The object is God's glory in Christ, but it is also your way to fully enjoy the new life. What is diligence? It is "haste" or "zeal"; a holy zeal for holiness.

Before the other graces of the Christian life can be realized, you must devote yourself to the new life with a holy zeal! We all devote ourselves to what is of first importance to us. Even the depressed individual is devoted. He devotes himself to feeling sorry for himself. Aren't you tired yet of the experts telling you that these people are not responsible for the irresponsible behavior to which they are devoted?

The first priority of the new life is the holy life. When a person enters the new life of Christian faith, why should he live according to the priorities of the old one? The freedom of holiness causes us to live this new life with diligence (zeal). Zeal does not mean frenzy or imbalance or fanaticism, though this is the popular idea of zeal. It means a devotion to the things that come from above, where the new life originates.

We are not called to some abstract, nebulous, or content-less zeal. Peter says that the application of diligence, this holy zeal we are talking about, is "in your faith." Faith is a gift (Eph. 2:8), but it is also something we exercise. Faith is not something that God does. Faith is a belief that God enables you to know and act upon in trusting His promise. God does not believe in Jesus Christ for you. You do that. You must receive, rest and rely on Jesus alone for salvation. This is not any kind of meritorious work. Christ's work on the cross is the only meritorious work there is. Entrusting yourself to Christ is not work. It is rest. Nonetheless, you must do it. You believe. Peter calls you to do it with a holy zeal. How does one believe with a holy zeal?

Abraham is an excellent example. "He believed in the Lord, and He reckoned it to him as righteousness" (Gen. 15:6 NASB). How did Abraham show he believed God? In Genesis 22:1–3 we read:

> Some time later God tested Abraham. He said to him, "Abraham!"
>
> "Here I am," he replied.
>
> Then God said, "Take your son, your only son Isaac, whom you love, and go to the region of Moriah. Sacrifice him there as a burnt offering on one of the mountains I will tell you about."
>
> Early the next morning Abraham got up and saddled his donkey.

In the most difficult moment of his life, knowing God's will, Abraham acted quickly. He arose "early" to do the unimaginable—kill his son—because God told him to. "Where is faith in all this," you ask? Everywhere! Abraham trusted God even in the face of the death of his only son. That was the depth of his trust. Isaac looked at him and said: "The fire and wood are here, but where is the lamb for the burnt offering? Abraham answered, 'God Himself will provide the lamb for the burnt offering, my son'" (Gen. 22:7, 8). This is faith! God will provide.

The writer of Hebrews also comments on this same phenomenon. In that great eleventh chapter concerning faith, he says, "Abraham reasoned that God could raise the dead, and figuratively speaking, he did receive Isaac back from death" (Heb. 11:19). This is the dynamic of faith. We believe that God is able to raise men, even from the dead.

Another example may help. Imagine that your house is burning down, and your children are on the top landing. You are on the ground floor crying out to them, "Jump!" What will save them? Some might say that faith is their believing I will catch them. This is just how much of the Christian community defines faith, as more of an intellectual acknowledgment. But is this "saving" faith? Could that sort of faith have saved the children? They could believe with all their heart that you would catch them, but if they didn't jump, they'd be dead.

What is saving faith in this example? It is the kind of believing that produces a jump. This kind of faith is not works. Instead, it is a "faith working through love" (Gal. 5:6 NASB). A faith that works acts like Abraham's faith. His faith propelled him out of Ur of the Chaldeans. This is a faith with Christ as its object, and it works through love with a holy zeal. But it does not stop there.

Faith works towards moral excellence or virtue. In the New Testament this word refers to more than just isolated deeds of moral excellence. It is a way of life. It is intimately connected to the man who sees he is responsible before a holy God. This idea of virtue is clearly linked with the perfection of God (2 Peter 1:3), but our lives are to demonstrate it as well (2 Peter 1:5).

Paul presents another picture of excellence in Philippians 4:8, the only place in his writings in which he uses this idea. Here is the goal that Christians should strive to attain.

This is demanding. Our goal is excellence—perfection! Perhaps this is why Peter describes us as those who have become "partakers of the divine nature" (2 Peter 1:4). This doesn't make us "little gods," but rather, those who have "escaped the corruption that is in the world by lust" (2 Peter 1:4 KJV), so that we now share the divine characteristic of moral or ethical purity.

It is instructive that Peter uses this idea of excellence first of God (v. 3) and later of men (v. 5). In the meantime we are to be removed from defilement and corruption and lust. We are to pursue the excellence that shows God is holy, by being holy in all we are and do.

This excellence, Peter says, is applied through knowledge of God. It is knowing and applying the truth. The New Testament understanding of knowledge involves our wills. Knowledge isn't just data to store away. It is the reality we act upon. The knowledge of God presupposes our ability to be excellent. When we aren't excellent, we are lying about God. That is why disobedience and sin in general is so serious. Even worse is to say that you are "unable to not sin." This is simply not true for a Christian. The call to perfection is not meant to break us, but to move us into that realm where the knowledge of God is continually infused into our lives. This brings us to an intimate connection with the next point: self-control.

Why, you might wonder, is self-control in a list of Christian virtues? It seems so inferior to knowledge or excellence. But it's not. Self-control is the organizing principle for a disciplined life. There is no godliness without self-control. Yet this is the stumbling block for many. For example, many continually "lose" their tempers. Others appear to be in total control and yet in stress wind up out of control in some kind of tantrum. Neither extreme represents a person who has self-control. Neither is excused for surrendering control, whether under small or great stress. In His grace, God has made it possible for His people to have mastery and control over themselves. What an extraordinary gift! All our excuses are gone, but how tightly we cling to them! How copiously we weep, all the while crying out, "I can't help it!" Of course we can! The problem is not our ability, but our desire. We desire (for a variety of reasons) to see ourselves as victims.

Years ago I counseled a woman who came close to taking her life. This was an intelligent woman with a beautiful family, a good job, a promising future, and a seemingly good relationship with Christ. Her job was difficult. There were pressures, but they were not unbearable. She kept telling herself that the "job was getting to her," and that she "couldn't cope." This led to "I'm worthless," which led to "I can't live." She then came within a hair's-breadth of ending it all, throwing away life, a family, everything—all because she believed the lie that she had no control over what was happening to her. Of course she did, even when she tried to end it all. How different we'd be if we used our control in godly ways instead of counter-productive and self-destructive ways.

We must persevere in self-control. Yes, we have control over ourselves, and that control is to be diligently applied at all times. That is how long it must operate. Perseverance means endurance, steadfastness, and brave patience. We are not to be cowards in the face of adversity.

Of course, this hits directly at the spirit of our age. We don't want to wait at all, let alone bravely! The new life is to be lived not with impulsively, but with brave patience. This is our need: "You need to persevere so that when you have done the will of God, you will receive what He has promised" (Heb. 10:36).

This brave patience is not for its own sake. In Romans 5:4 we read that perseverance produces "proven character." God is concerned to prove our characters. All the struggles we face are meant to conform us more and more to the image of Christ in a life of active obedience and worship.

This active obedience demands love for others. We begin with those nearest to us, and then reach out to the world. We must take notice of their situations, failings, and successes, while being compassionate and helpful. The freedom we have in Christ is not self-oriented. Jesus said, "If you love me, you will keep my commandments" (John 14:15 NASB). Love for our brothers is not an option; it is a commandment—a commandment with an example. We are to love our brothers as Christ loved us" (John 15:12). He loved us in a way that at every step went against himself. It was total giving. It was sacrificial. While it brought Him death, it brings us life.

Our love for our brethren is only a horizontal picture of an even greater quality in the new life. We are to love doubly—in two, often parallel, kinds of love placed side by side. It is as though He says, "Add love to your love." As Paul states so eloquently in 1 Corinthians 13, "the greatest of these is love."

Peter is saying the same thing in his own way. Your self-control can be contrived and your endurance can be stoic, but undergirding it all is a reality that can never be contrived or simply philosophical. Love is total. It is the giving of yourself in spite of yourself! To demonstrate this love, you must focus on Christ, who is the perfect example of such enduring, giving, caring love. This is what makes us new men. It is a new love in which we are taken over by God and in which our wills are subdued by Him, and submitted to Him, moment by moment, day by day. We are liberated to love!

The freedom to which we have been called can only complete itself in love. We are called to follow Him to the end (perseverance) under any obstacle (self-control) with a clear vision of His purpose (knowledge) as people who shine as lights in a dark world (virtue). This is what the Christian life is all about. This is what it means to be a new creature. It is the radical newness of those who leave everything to follow and love Him with a passionate devotion. We do this as part of a new community of brotherly love, which has renounced hatred and bitterness so that we might love others, just as He first loved us (1 John 4:19).

People want certainty in their lives. Christians want assurance as well. They want to know that God is real and that their place is safe in Him. Peter concludes this section with these words of the assurance we so desperately crave: "For if you possess these qualities in increasing measure, they will keep you from being ineffective and unproductive in your knowledge of our Lord Jesus Christ" (2 Peter 1:8). Living the new life brings its own assurance. The joy and freedom of the Christian life is always available, but it is only available as we live in obedience to Him. This is the clear and simple message of the Bible.

Study Guide

1. What is the relationship between being "alive in Christ" and actually experiencing new life in Christ?

2. Do you believe that you have everything you need to live a godly life? If not, what else do you think you need? Is it ever someone else's fault when you sin?

3. What does it mean to devote ourselves to the new life with diligence and zeal? What would that look like in your own life?

4. If faith is a gift, how do we also exercise our faith? What do we learn from the example of Abraham's faith?

5. If new life in Christ calls us to perfection, or excellence, what are some areas in your life where you accept mediocrity? Do you pursue excellence in loving the brethren? In self-control?

22

Freedom to Remain Shackled: Its Consequences and Costs

*T*he new life is a day-by-day unfolding of the joyful, strength-ening life and freedom found in the love of God. It is a con-tinual unfolding of a new and splendid righteousness that marks our being. We might assume that all people (especially Christians) want this freedom to live righteously, but nothing could be farther from the truth. Look around you! People everywhere are weighed down by a life of complaints, unhap-piness, bitterness, envy, jealousy and gossip. You might say, "No one could want that kind of life!" Then why are most people living this way?

People are not living this way by chance. Millions of people each moment decide to live with complaints and envy. How many people do you think actually face a trial-filled moment and pause to remember, "This is an opportunity to glorify You, O God"? How many people regard someone who has more than they, and pray that the Lord will bless them more? We squander our time and energy by hating others for having more than we. We resent God for holding back abundance from us, thereby losing what we do have and squandering what we are. We rarely appreciate our situation. We choose to hope in a future that doesn't exist, rather than to live for God in the present that He has given us. Soon, we think, we will be better—but we are never better enough. Soon we will have more, but we never have enough.

Perhaps you are looking at the title of the chapter and wondering, "How is this freedom?" It is the freedom to imprison yourself. You see, you are free to live this way, self-shackled and complaining, morose and bitter. I can't take this freedom away from you. I can tell you, though, how obnoxious and dishonoring to God it is. God won't change it. Change is up to you.

Of course, God has made it possible for you to change, but the decision to do so remains in your hands. People refuse to change because, on some level within their personal decision-making apparatus, this is the most satisfactory choice. In other words, it is (as they size it up) the most rewarding way to live.

Biblically speaking, it is slavery. Theoretically, every Christian would denounce these patterns. Yet, they tenaciously persist. Test yourself. See how much time you spent yesterday not thinking about your present gifts and opportunities, or about what was positive, constructive and glorifying to God. You worried about how much money you needed for something, but didn't have. You worried about someone's wrong assessment of you, or how unfair it was that someone other than you had the job, promotion, house, car, wife, etc.. How much energy was spent putting down others?

I asked a group of people in the congregation that I pastor to do an experiment. I asked them to commit themselves to one week without gossip. I actually felt a bit foolish requesting one week of a behavior that is supposed to be permanent. But I knew that they, like most others, engaged in gossip at times, and it wasn't enough to say, "Don't gossip." I wanted them to see clearly to what extent gossip was a part of their lives. They came back a week later, astounded. Some of them felt that almost their entire conversation had ceased.

This is incredibly revealing. We are choosing (even as committed Christians) behavior that accomplishes nothing worthwhile and destroys others and self, yet we continue. Gossip is a kind of friendship that you and the person with whom you are gossiping share at the expense of the subject of your gossip. Together you approve of yourselves because you are superior to the one about whom you gossip.

You may see yourself in yet another example. How do you view the prosperous members of your church? Isn't it easy to envy them, even piously? By that I mean it is easy to disguise our envy as piety: "A real Christian doesn't have much. Joe Smith has a lot. He can't be a real Christian. I have a little. I'm a better Christian than he is."

In our hearts we don't like the idea that someone has more than we do. We may not want to work harder, but we hate not having things, especially when others do. So we find ways to make them seem less worthy than us, in spite of their honest achievements. We even misinterpret the Bible to make our point. "Woe to you rich," we say. We are not concerned for the souls of the rich; we simply envy them for what they have. We make excuses for our anger against God's providence and perhaps for our own laziness or carelessness.

Those whose poverty results from a biblically directed life will not hate, envy, or malign those who have chosen another godly way. How easily we forget that riches or poverty are not ultimately important. Rather, James says, "Let the rich man glory in his humiliation" (James 1:10 KJV). Our attitude towards what we have should reflect Paul's who said, "I know how to get along with humble means, and I also know how to live in prosperity" (Phil. 4:12 NASB). Paul saw God's hand in every circumstance of life. He did not make circumstances an excuse for envy or any other sin.

Examples abound. People live their lives depressed. They believe they are depressed for some reason beyond their control, therefore it is "right." They believe they are not to be blamed when people dislike their behavior. They lose friends and alienate others as sympathy turns to frustration and frustration to anger. Then they condemn their former friends and family because they will no longer indulge their miserable self-absorption. All this is used to reinforce the necessity of being depressed.

In 1942–1944, a young girl had her life devastated by the ravages of war. She spent her fourteenth and fifteenth years locked in a tiny hiding place with seven other people. Anne Frank certainly could have chosen bitterness. She could have viewed her life as wasted. The seven others locked up with her did. Here is her assessment:

> I am young and I possess many buried qualities; I am young and strong and am living a great adventure; I am still in the midst of it and can't grumble the whole day long. I have been given a lot, a happy nature, a great deal of cheerfulness and strength. Every day I feel that I am developing inwardly, that the liberation is drawing nearer and how beautiful nature is [she had not been outside those rooms for two years!] how interesting this adventure is! Why then should I be in despair? . . . [Yet I] see nothing but dissatisfied, grumpy faces here, nothing but sighs and suppressed complaints; it really would seem as if suddenly we were very badly off here. *If the truth is told, things are just as bad as you yourself care to make them.* [Emphasis mine] There's no one here that sets a good example; everyone should see that he gets the better of his own moods. Every day you hear, "If only it was all over." My work, my hope, my love, my courage, all these things keep my head above water and keep me from complaining.[1]

Like Anne Frank, we are all going to die. Everyone! Each person from her room died with her in death camps except her father. They didn't have many choices, but they did have one: They could choose how they would live life while awaiting death.

Christians especially should live cheerfully as they face death, because they have been given faith, hope, and perseverance. We cannot always control our circumstances, but we can control ourselves. We can't control our end, but we can control (at least to a degree) how we arrive there. A story may clarify my meaning.

An old trapper was caught in an early-winter blizzard in Northern Canada. The wind chill factor was minus 40 degrees Celsius, and he felt he couldn't go on. From out of nowhere he saw a light. He noticed more lights and realized he had reached a settlement. Just when he thought he was home free, he found himself separated from the settlement by a frozen river. There was no way around it. Yet, if he stayed where he was, it meant certain death. Since it was early winter, he reasoned that the ice might not support him. He had no choice but to try, and no time to waste. He began by walking gingerly. The ice held. As he got further out, he thought he heard cracking ice. He got down on his knees and moved by inches. He was near the center. Even in the bitter cold he was drenched with sweat. The terror of plunging to an icy, frozen death in the black waters of this northern river gripped him. He got down on his face. Now he was in danger of hypothermia, as the arctic cold froze his fear-sweat. He had to be patient, moving by inches. With time running out he continued to move with agonizing slowness to the other side. What was left of life became dreamlike.

Suddenly, he heard bells. "Could it be? Do I hear bells?" He did. The sound grew louder, now he heard horses coming towards him and the sound of a wagon. There was singing. The sound came from behind him until it seemed to be upon him. He turned and within feet of him was a logging sleigh being drawn by a team of horses. The bells made music and the driver was singing. He knew then that the ice was solid. He jumped up and ran safely to the other side.

This story has a moral. Both the sleigh driver and the trapper made it to the other side. The only difference was how they got there. All true Christians will make it to the other side, but how will they get there? Will they choose to scrape along inch by inch in fear and terror, or will they arrive singing and laughing and rejoicing? This is the choice for you, Christian. You are free to be shackled in sin, but true freedom comes in living a life of unbounded, daily joy. Let us now take a look at this freedom and joy that God gives to His people.

Endnotes

1. Anne Frank, *The Dairy of a Young Girl,* Doubleday, 1958, pp. 188, 101.

Study Guide

1. Consider a Christian, perhaps even yourself, who is not living in the freedom of the new life. What's really stopping them from changing? How have they been deceived into remaining shackled?

2. Read Philippians 4:12. If Paul knew how to get along in humble circumstances; do you? How do you find strength in Christ in moments of struggle and difficulty?

3. What was so unusual about Anne Frank? Given that we're all going to die, how will you choose to live while awaiting death?

23

Freedom In Joy

I am a pastor in the Reformed Presbyterian Church. This church, which became known as the Covenanter Church, originated in Scotland where its faith was demonstrated in the 1680s during what became known as the "killing times." During those years, thousands of Scottish Covenanters were killed for their faith. Those times demanded intense commitment, sober living, and clear-headed purpose. This church, by God's grace, has remained faithful and biblical, but they are not known for their joy. This doesn't necessarily mean Reformed Presbyterians have no joy; they just do not always show it.

A little example may help. A man told me of visiting one of our remaining Scottish Covenanter churches while on vacation. He was moved by the service and deeply convicted during the preaching. At a certain point, unable to contain himself, he shouted out, "Praise the Lord!" At that point, a man in front of him turned and with a glower said, "Excuse me! We don't praise the Lord around here!" I think for many Christians and many Christian churches, that could be the motto: "We don't praise the Lord around here." The point is simple. God doesn't call us to spew forth mindless "Praise the Lords." At the same time, our walk with God is not meant to be dour, morose, or praiseless.

The fruit of the Spirit includes joy (Gal. 5:22), and the essential fruit of the Spirit is love (Gal. 5:6). Love's first offspring is joy. A love-filled life is a joy-filled life. John Calvin, whose portraits seem to reflect stern coldness, says of this passage that the "joy does not here, I think, denote that joy in the Holy Ghost (Rom. 14:17) of which he [Paul] speaks elsewhere, but that cheerful behavior towards our fellow-man, which is the opposite of moroseness."

Cheerfulness instead of moroseness. What have you brought your family, your friends, your colleagues today? Did you bring good cheer? Or did you bring gloom, complaints and profanity?

When I first became a Christian, I had to give up many ridiculous activities and sins. I had never been serious about anything. Now for the first time I became serious. Seriousness is praiseworthy but I became morose, thinking I was being serious. I gave up sin but I also gave up laughter. I was defensive and uptight in my new faith and always on guard for the attack aimed at it. One day Jay Adams firmly commanded me: "Rich, be of good cheer!" then he said, "Jesus commanded you to be of good cheer."

I wonder how many of us have forgotten that liberating command, "Be of good cheer" (John 16:33 KJV). It all fits together when we hear Christ's reason, "because I have overcome the world" (John 16:33). The victory is won. What are we dragging, sagging and moaning about? Christ has beaten His and our adversary. Christ has borne our punishment, destroyed the power of sin, and conquered death for us. All this must bring us good cheer.

Joy, a fruit of the Spirit, is an indication of our fellowship with God. It is our privilege to be cheerful, even in difficult straits. He has already taken care of the problem for us. Trust enables you to live not only in faith, but in faith with joy. Nothing needs to remove your joy. Not one of the many minor "catastrophes" and inconveniences or great real-life tragedies that come to all. This doesn't mean you should rejoice because of tragedy or suffering. It doesn't mean you are always to be happy. Indeed you will sorrow and grieve, "but not as those who have no hope" (1 Thess 4:13). Yet in all things you can choose the peace of resting, abiding, and hoping in Christ, who brings joy—even in your worst tribulations.

Study Guide

1. Have you ever been in a Christian community where expressions of joy were not welcome? Is it necessary to show joy in our walk with Christ?

2. Read Galatians 5:22–23. If joy is one of the fruits of the Spirit, why are we often content to live as Christians without it?

3. Think about a joyful Christian you know. What kinds of attitudes, words and actions characterize his or her life?

4. What is the difference between happiness and joy? On what fact or circumstance is each based?

24

Freedom from Hopeless Bondage to Sin:
A Case Study

Sue, her husband Fred, and their small child attended a morning worship service in our congregation. Almost as soon as the benediction was pronounced, they were heading out the door. When new people come to our assembly and then attempt to flee immediately, I hasten after them to introduce myself and find out what brought them (or who sent them). Actually, Sue and Fred were not too hasty in making their getaway. They were slow enough to be caught.

People referred to our church often have problems and are in desperate need of help. It has been my experience that these "runners" are not really running away, but calling attention to themselves, hoping for a caring response.

As I walked toward them, I noticed how slowly they were gathering themselves together. They were reserved, shy, and hesitant. I asked them what brought them and they mentioned the name of a friend who does counseling. I knew then that this was a "counseling" couple. They weren't there for worship, but for help. How long would it be before they told me their purpose?

Fred asked me how I spent my time during the week. I explained that I taught at a seminary, did numerous Bible studies and was involved in much counseling. I asked why he was interested and he said it was because they might like to speak to me. We set up a time and began meeting that week.

They told me that Sue was an alcoholic. She had been raised in a Christian home, but she met and married Fred, who was not a Christian. From that point on, she had the perfect excuse for her lack of commitment, her lack of church attendance, and many other sins in her life: Fred was not a Christian!

Sue told me that if only Fred had been interested in Christianity, none of this would have happened to her. A pattern began to emerge. Things "happened" to her, but she was never in control, never really responsible. I took her at her word (1 Cor. 13:7). We began to explore two areas: her drinking and Fred's rejection of Christianity. I had one condition. If they wanted to see me, they had to continue to worship with us. I explained that an hour a week with me, even with homework, was not enough. They needed regular involvement with the body of God's people.

Breaking deep-seated sinful habit patterns involves a restructuring that is greatly helped by the local church. If people won't agree to this condition, I encourage them to deal with their problems and find a church in which they will be helped. When people are already involved in other Bible-believing churches, I encourage them to seek help from their own pastors and elders. After all, that is their job. If they can't, I offer free courses in biblical counseling open to pastors. If people are not Christians, I always present the Gospel to them as the way of help and of hope.

Fred was deeply interested in Christianity. He began to read the Bible and study it. He had all kinds of questions. He came not only to the worship services, but to the midweek Bible study as well. At this point, Sue began to complain that Fred seemed only interested in the Bible. The situation clarified. Soon, only

Fred came to the worship services. Sue always had an excuse—too busy, too tired, too something or other.

Not only did Sue stop coming, but she went out of her way to find fault with the church. Then Fred made a serious commitment to Christ. We talked of baptism. Sue tried to dissuade him. She said that she had heard there were points in our church's constitution with which her grandfather disagreed. However, her father visited and rejoiced that his daughter had found a church and that his son-in-law had found Christ. He had no idea how strenuously his daughter was fighting Christ.

Why would Sue claim for six years that her husband's lack of Christian commitment was her problem, and then fly into a rage when her husband became committed to Christ and involved in the church?

Sue believed that she was a fine Christian woman, that her husband's unbelief was her stumbling block, and that if only he were a Christian, she would be okay. Why all the pretense? Simply because Sue, like millions of other alcoholics, will do anything to protect her drinking. Alcoholics will destroy homes and marriages, lie, cheat, steal, ruin careers, and even sell family treasures for the next drink. There is nothing in the life of an alcoholic that is sacred, except the next drink. The deepest lie Sue told herself was that she didn't really need to drink and that she could quit whenever she wanted.

Following Fred's conversion, Sue began to drink more. Just prior to Fred's baptism, Sue was drunk more than she was sober. Soon I realized that Sue had no desire to receive counsel from me. She acted as though she was in control of everything and needed no help at all. The counseling developed into a strong confrontation between an enraged Sue and me as her counselor, who wouldn't let her escape responsibility. For six years Fred had kept her drinking secret. He had sheltered and hidden her sin. No one confronted her. Now for the first time in our meetings, Sue was being confronted head-on.

Sue would sit down and immediately begin weeping. I would ask her to stop. She would say that she couldn't, that she was helpless to control her tears. I would tell her that she used tears to manipulate people, that with her tears she was really saying, "Please don't hurt me, I'm just a poor, helpless little girl." Then her tears would stop and she would stare at me with angry eyes. I would go on, saying "Whether you cry or not, your tears will not stop me. You use them not only to manipulate, but as a defense, a wall, to keep people away. I'm not staying away. Neither is Fred. Neither is the church."

Finally one day, Sue wept at church and said she was repentant. Since she now claimed to be prepared to change her life, I asked her if that meant she was prepared to go to Alcoholics Anonymous meetings.

Now, there is nothing magical about AA meetings. They are not Christian meetings, but Christians can profit from the multiple confrontations that take place there. More than anything else, I was interested if she was prepared to openly deal with her sinful habit pattern of drunkenness.

I asked her about AA, not because of my complete approval of it, but more because of her continual and persistent refusal to attend meetings. Her refusal had signaled to me that she was afraid of those who were determined to rip her bottle away. My challenge to her was simply a test. Was she truly willing to do anything God would ask of her? She had become happy in the church when she attended, but that was because they were supportive, rather than confrontational. She needed numerous people confronting her as I was.

I had assigned Sue a mentor, a former alcoholic, but she avoided the mentor just as she had avoided me. Sue would say of her, "She's too simplistic," or "She doesn't believe I'm a Christian," or "She keeps waiting for me to make a commitment to Christ, when I'm already a Christian." Following her so-called repentance, she wouldn't even speak to this member and she wouldn't continue her meetings with me. "I've got it now; what do I need to speak to you for?" was her attitude.

Eventually Sue agreed to a counseling session, but she called an hour before our meeting to announce that there were problems with the car. When I persisted in asking what the car problem was, she confessed that she was so terrified of coming to the meeting that she was sure she'd crack up the car. She said she wouldn't come. I told her that coming or not was her decision and I refused to blame it on her car, her terrors, me or anything else. I also told her that she managed every day as she headed into town to purchase her daily supply of alcohol. That ended the call.

I knew that everything was coming to a breaking point. When the meeting time arrived, both she and her husband were there. I opened by telling her that the only reason I had scheduled the meeting was because I had believed her report of repentance. I told her that I had no desire to coerce anyone into receiving counseling from me, and since I had learned that her public repentance had been short lived, this would be our final meeting. We would meet again when she was prepared to do whatever God would have her do.

In the midst of her tears and anger, I suggested that regardless of her words and protests to the contrary, she was continuing to do exactly what she wanted to, which was to drink. I continued by saying that as long as drinking was what she wanted most, that is exactly what she would do. I expected a rash of protests. I expected her to complain that I was judging her, which would have been accurate. Instead, she simply said, "of course." Baffled, I asked her what she meant. She told me that she prayed regularly for God to make her "not want to drink." It never happened, and so she thought that God understood that she had to drink, since He had not yet made her not want to. She had been unwilling to go to AA for the same reason. How could anyone except God make her not want this? And until God made her not want to, she believed her drunkenness was completely understandable, and acceptable.

I nearly leapt from my seat. I directed her to the seventh chapter of Romans. I read how Paul didn't do what he wanted to do, and did what he didn't want to do. With those words, Sue experienced a deep kinship with Paul, who even after twenty

Christian years still experienced the wretchedness of giving in to sin he didn't want to do.

It amazed Sue that the "great" Paul still sinned, while wanting righteousness. What was most eye opening to Sue was that God had never taken the wanting of sin away from Paul. The next revelation brought liberty and freedom to Sue.

I pointed out that Paul's glory was not that he didn't ever want to sin, but that in spite of intense carnal pressures and temptations to engage in sin, he didn't. Paul's strength was Christ. Christ had filled him with the Spirit. The Spirit promised sanctification—not the removal of his desires. Paul was declared righteous because of Christ's righteousness. He was being sanctified by God's grace, not by his sudden removal from temptation.

I pointed out to Sue that she didn't have to wait until she didn't want to drink any more. In spite of everything inside her demanding release in drunkenness, she could choose not to sin. God would give her the strength to overcome.

Sue had never thought that she could stop sinning, and she began living righteously. Drunkenness and its host of related sins had claimed a huge hold on her life, threatening ruin, and she thought she was stuck with it.

Sue has begun that new daily walk of faith, in which she is thinking about and doing what is right in spite of all the pressures to the contrary. Day by day she is experiencing the freedom of a child of God, who thought she had to "feel righteous" before she could act and be righteous.

There are many people like Sue who believe they are hopelessly bound to sin. This is not true, but it leads to one of the biggest controversies in Christianity. Was the answer for Sue that God does everything? Was the answer for Sue that she had to do everything for sanctification, for overcoming sin, for living righteously? Neither scenario is the answer. How do we integrate what God "does" and what we "do" as we seek to live the Christian life free from the misery of sin? This question is the focus of the next chapter.

Study Guide

1. Have you ever broken a deep seated, sinful habit pattern by yourself? What was the role of Christian friends, pastors, and the church body in this process?

2. What kind of approach must a counselor take when dealing with someone committed to long-standing sinful habit patterns?

3. What do you think of Alcoholics Anonymous? As a non-Christian organization, what can we learn from it? What sort of assumptions must we be careful not to accept?

4. Read Romans 7:15–25. Does God have to change our desires before we can actually change?

5. When people believe that they are hopelessly bound to sin, what do they need to understand? How does the promise of sanctification help a person mired in life-destroying habit patterns?

25

Freedom: Responsibility versus Sovereignty

*T*here is perhaps nothing more essential for blessing and freedom in the Christian life than understanding both that God is absolutely sovereign, and that we are completely responsible before Him for all our actions. This balance eludes many Christians because they never seem to appreciate that the balance actually exists.

People talk with disdain about extremists. The truth of the matter is that most of us are extremists. If we believe something is true, we won't let ourselves believe that something else may possibly be true. This is not only so for Christians, but non-Christians as well. Atheists, for example, deride even the very idea of God. This is especially true of people mired in cults. Try to argue a Jehovah's Witness out of his view that neither Jesus nor the Holy Spirit is God. In a recent confrontation I had with one, even though I used his Bible and pointed out numerous references, he wouldn't budge. At first I suspected he was brainwashed, but it was more subtle than that. He was an extremist who had found his extreme, and reality notwithstanding, he was going to stay there.

It is the same in Christian circles. Just mention predestination and it is as though you have declared war. People forget everything else and are ready for battle. One side defends God's sovereignty (as it is demonstrated in His election of His people), while the other side defends man's freedom. All the while the whole church suffers—and not just from doctrinal deficiency, but from failing to know and experience God rightly and fully.

Why is it necessary to understand the biblical balance of God's sovereignty and man's responsibility? The biblical balance will bring a true knowledge of God, which will bring greater enjoyment of Him and our life on earth. I am convinced that only as we rightly understand the biblical teachings on God's sovereignty can we truly have the enjoyment and freedom in our lives that Christ's death has procured. The doctrines of God's sovereignty and man's responsibility bring us to the heart of God, while at the same time piercing the heart of man.

When we understand this balance, we will understand the choices we make. If we are robots, then it really doesn't matter what we choose. It doesn't matter if I spend my life as a thief or as a philanthropist. So then, resolving this question will help us to understand whether we are meaningful beings or not.

Interestingly, evolutionists decry our belief in God. They say we are just chance accumulations of molecules that have emerged on the basis of time plus chance. This philosophy makes man nothing. As Skinner says in Beyond Freedom and Dignity, "to man as man I happily say, 'Good riddance.'" Yet it is precisely these individuals who, by their philosophical destruction of God and man, are left with a meaningless world, which at the same time elevates man to the status of a god. This is the paradox of the humanist movement. Man, the chance accumulation of cells, must now save himself. They don't ever seem to see the irony of their position.

The Christian theological world hasn't helped much in clarifying this issue. What they have done is to make this basic issue one of "either/or." Man is backed into a corner. To choose God means to excuse man and to choose man has led to excluding God. The consequences on both sides have been disastrous.

What does it do for a Christian's life to walk around as though nothing he does matters? He'll do nothing that matters. Conversely, what is the result of living as though each person's eternal destiny (including your own) ultimately depends on himself? It cripples him.

Living as though man's choice is supreme is deficient theology with respect to God. Theologians have battled this back and forth since Paul. Paul understood that the resolution wasn't found in an "either/or" situation, but instead upheld the two great poles of the Christian life: the sovereignty of God and the full responsibility of man. People, because of their own sin, have chosen one or the other, but the route to blessedness and freedom is to understand the two in tension and balance.

This tension is seen most clearly in Philippians 2:12–13, where Paul places both poles together: "Work out your salvation with fear and trembling, for it is God who is at work in you, both to will and to work for His good pleasure" (NASB). This call is a great responsibility—to engage ourselves totally (even with our emotions) in the salvation that God has given to His people. There is no slacking off here. All that God puts before us is important. Our lives, our work, and our battles are important.

Those who stop there are wrong. You can work out your salvation for one reason alone, and that reason is not the dignity or nobility of man. It is rather because "God is at work in you both to will and to work for His good pleasure." What a wonderful truth! We can be fully, engagingly, passionately responsible in our world, because He is at work in us.

However, there is more to the promise. God is not just in us; he is in His people for a two-fold purpose: "both to will and to work for His good pleasure." In other words, God's presence in His people enables them to will, as well as to do. Those who speak of "free will" speak of it as an entity outside the control of God. This is not the case at all! God causes us to will. Some may find that discouraging or disheartening. "We want our own wills!" they shout, but should we be in love with an autonomous will? Should we want any part of our lives to be excluded from the power of God? Isn't it only pride that exalts a so-called "free will" rather than pleading for a God-controlled and God-centered will? You would be amazed at how different you would be if you acknowledged the supremacy of God not only for your actions, but also for your wills. You'd be amazed at how much your actions would change and your freedom would deepen.

This does not mean you will no longer take responsibility. Now your responsibility will not be sovereign, but subordinate. And your God will no longer be an appendage to your choice, but the Supreme Counselor of your life.

Study Guide

1. Have you ever experienced the tension between God's sovereignty and man's responsibility? Why is it necessary to understand the biblical balance? How might an imbalance on either side lead to a lack of true freedom?

2. Read Philippians 2:12–13. How does this passage help us to balance divine sovereignty and human responsibility? Paul says that God is working in his people for what two-fold purpose?

3. What is the role of human pride in exalting "free will"? Should we want any of our lives excluded from God's sovereign will?

26

Freedom and Conspiracy: Man's Quest for Personal Freedom

*T*he Christian grows in understanding freedom as he grows in knowledge of sin. One characteristic of sin is that it is conspiratorial. While the contents of sinful conspiracies vary, one constant is the "alternate covenant proposal." You see, at creation, God created man in a covenantal relationship with Himself. Man could have been bound to obey God solely by reason of his createdness, but instead, God graciously relates to him by way of a covenant. Whether he is a covenant-keeper or a covenant-breaker does not change the covenant; it only changes the status of the relationship. Thus man's nature is inescapably covenant-seeking. When sin enters the world, man refuses to honor his covenant with God and seeks another covenant designed to replace God's covenant. This demonstrates the conspiratorial nature of sin, as it diabolically replicates the covenantal nature of man. Conspiracies are essentially wicked covenants.

There has always been one enduring covenant between man and God. Through many administrations and several mediators, it has remained essentially the same. Over time, the covenant became more complex, but it was not replaced. In its final form with Christ as Mediator, all the provisions of the covenant are fulfilled. In spite of complexities that we may not understand, the covenanting activity of the righteous secures order and peace, by the grace and goodness of God. The covenanting of the wicked, on the other hand, produces chaos. Conspiracies always disappear in turbulence. They are replaced with multiplying conspiracies, which conspire against each other. Hence war and rumors of war.

One of the great conspiracies against God's covenant in our time is dedicated to the ideal of "personal freedom." Sinners have conspired together and covenanted to create an order in which all individuals are free to follow their own desires, to be a law unto themselves. This conspiracy would seem to be the end of law, but actually it is a reduction of all laws to one: "Let your neighbor be."

The problem is that in order for this conspiracy to work, the population of the world would need to be reduced to the point where no man would interact with another. Hence, the conspiracy is impractical and cannot be implemented. To realize the conspiracy, opponents must be liquidated, thus contradicting the ideal of the conspiracy. Along the way, the ideal of individualism must be continually modified and the goal of absolute personal freedom must be surrendered. The new goal must be the "maximization of personal freedom." New agreements on the limits of personal freedom continually erode the ideal of personal freedom. Those who can not agree to the limits find that they have no personal freedom in a society where personal freedom is idealized.

Christians, God's covenantally faithful people, have often been seduced by the ideal of personal freedom. In some circles, personal freedom is even thought to be a Christian doctrine—though it is really an anti-covenantal idea, of demonic origin. This dogma is held across all denominational lines, including liberals and fundamentalists. The ideal of personalistic humanism has been adopted and adapted by virtually all religious groups. Religious differences and allegiances are debated, with the merits of each decided by how it is perceived to implement the ideal of personal freedom. This state of affairs has encouraged a distrust of and opposition to all institutions. All claims of authority over individuals are resisted or denied. The family and state enforcement of lawful contracts, the institutions upon which civilization has depended, are disappearing. Where Christians are involved, the spirit of anti-authority is directed towards the church as well.

The Christian solution for the present anarchic, disintegrating, dehumanizing situation is not authoritarianism from the church. Authoritarianism involves endowing of any person or human institution with absolute authority. (thus the absolutizing of personal freedom is itself a form of authoritarianism!) God alone is sovereign, so all institutions of human authority must be denied total authority.

The Christian church is an institution of God with Jesus Christ as its sovereign King. The King has delegated limited exercise of His sovereign authority to his ministers. These constitute the government of the church. As ministers of Christ, the government of the church has real authority over the members of the church in the exercise of the authority Christ delegated. The church on earth is correctly described as a human institution with divine authority. It has an ordained organization and infrastructure.

Other God-ordained human institutions with delegated authority are the family and the state. Just like the family and the state, the church's authority is a visible reality—yet it differs from other institutions in one obvious way. God has not granted the church permission to enforce even its proper authority by physical force. The church depends upon the Spirit to enforce its authority over its members. The church is thus limited to preaching, warning, exhortation and pronouncements when dealing with the disobedient. In short, the church appeals to the conscience, and the Spirit makes the appeal effective.

The church, like all other institutions of human authority, may not make primary law. Primary law is covenant law, and it is proclaimed in Scripture. Secondary law is necessary law made consistent with primary law, with whatever restrictions have been placed on its administrative authority by God. In one sense, secondary law is simply the implementation of God's primary law. Nevertheless, secondary law has the force of law when proclaimed by lawful institutions in a lawful way. Thus, the implementation of God's law for its members by a lawful church comes with a powerful moral demand upon the consciences of its members. The first reaction of the Christian must be nearly reflexive obedience to the authority of the church. Such obedience should also mark of our lives in the family and the state, as well as the church.

The conscience is never bound absolutely by the secondary dictates of lawful institutions of human authority. This includes the church. All such human institutions are subject to sin. They do err. Therefore, exceptional cases may arise in which the individual conscience must resist secondary law. The Christian must be alert to several possibilities in order that he may "obey God rather than men." First, laws of human institutions may be intrinsically sinful, clearly contradicting God's Law. These are the easiest cases. Here the Christian should have no doubt about his proper action. Conscience demands that the sinful decree not be obeyed. Of course, his conscience must not be an arrogant conscience that thinks more highly of itself than it ought to think. The Christian conscience is informed by the Word of God. It is a reasonable conscience with a teachable spirit.

The hard case comes when the thing commanded by the lawful human authority is not intrinsically sinful. It may even be something the Christian regards as expedient for the sake of Christ under the circumstances. However, problems arise when the lawful authority exceeds its authority. If God has granted freedom to the individual in a particular matter, is it sinful to surrender that freedom—if freedom itself is the only consideration? Is it not possible to make an idol out of freedom, just as we can make an idol out of any good gift of God?

Our first impulse must be to obey lawful authority in the absence of an overwhelming reason not to obey. The individual ought to hesitate long before he determines that disobedience is necessary in the name of freedom. One consequence of disobedience, whether intended or not, is to weaken the force of lawful authority. In a sinful world, the position of lawful authority is at least as precarious as lawful freedom. When should one disobey for the sake of freedom? One should do so, if one is convinced the principle of freedom is endangered. At that point, one should insist on one's freedom, lest freedom be destroyed as an active principle of Christian life. Putting it another way, I would disobey if the demand for obedience were grounded in authoritarianism, or if the threat of authoritarianism was a clear and present danger.

Jesus' handling of the temple tax in Matthew 17:24–27 provides a good illustration. He said "the sons are exempt" from paying the temple tax (v. 26). "But so that we may not offend them . . . give it to them for my tax and yours" (v. 27). Jesus taught us that freedom need not always be claimed, but may be surrendered for the sake of the Kingdom of God.

The humanist ideal of personal freedom works to tear man from a covenantal relationship and dependence upon God. We must cease from being seduced by this idol, which like the golden calf (Exo. 32) has been raised up before us as the god who delivered us from bondage. In the Christian camp, the idol of personal freedom is often labeled "Christian liberty." But in fact, the biblical freedom of the Christian has nothing to do with the modern notion of personal freedom. The answer to the conspiracy of personal freedom is not authoritarianism, but covenant life with due respect for the divinely instituted structures of authority, guarded by a deep reverence for God with a constant readiness to submit unconditionally to Him. Let us now look at those in obedient covenant life.

Study Guide

1. As you have grown in your understanding of freedom, have you also grown in your knowledge of sin? Why or why not?

2. How does the covenantal nature of the gospel enable you to see your sin without despairing?

3. Sin conspires against God's covenant by counterfeiting it. How has our society replicated a wicked covenant based on "personal responsibility"? What are some of the consequences of this view?

4. What is the difference between the authority of the state and the authority of the church? Must every Christian be obedient to all that the state or his own church demands? When should one disobey for the sake of freedom?

5. Read Matthew 17:24–27. How does Jesus' teaching on the Kingdom of God help us to understand the relationship between church and state?

27

Who is Free?

Jesus said, "If the Son sets you free, you will be free indeed" (John 8:36). This could be translated, "If the Son sets you free, you will be really free." Who is this person who is really free? It is the Christian. The believer, Jesus says, is really free. This, of course, is not what our world calls "personal freedom." It is a condition of covenant living under King Jesus.

A superficial analysis of the Christian community might conclude, "These people are not really free." Even a deeper look might confirm this assessment. But is it accurate? No, it is not. The real people of God are "really" free, in spite of how they look. However, though they have made the commitment that brings freedom, they rarely use it fully. Why? Because they expect their commitment to Christ, which brings eternal life, also to bring them all the blessings now. Our commitment to Christ brings many blessings now, but the victory of the Christian life is not entirely realized with our initial commitment.

As a young Christian, the great freedom of living in Christ was, for the most part, a mystery to me. Oh, I heard many pious platitudes, like "Just let go and let God" and "You have to die to yourself."

The world has its formulas as well. John Lennon declared that "All you [really] need is love." Carl Rogers, the guru of the Human Potential movement, said the same thing. Glasser, the pioneer of Reality Therapy, claimed you needed responsibility.

Jesus says we need the Son. Paul says we need Him from beginning to end (Phil. 1:6). This "really free" life is not just an abstraction or a vague possibility. It is a full-fledged possibility open to all of Christ's people, available at any time. And if you know one of Christ's disciples who is really free, you can observe it. What then are the marks of someone who is really free?

1. **Really free people know.** They know they have been redeemed by the blood of Jesus Christ. They know their sins are forgiven. They know they have eternal life. This "knowing" undergirds their conscious experience of life.

2. **Really free people live.** They live out of what they know. They don't plan to live, they live! They don't live or not live according to whether their fortunes are good or bad. They live as masters of their situations. Remember Paul:

   > I am not saying this because I am in need, for I have learned to be content whatever the circumstances. I know what it is to be in need, and I know what it is to have plenty. I have learned the secret of being content in any and every situation, whether well fed or hungry, whether living in plenty or in want. I can do everything through Him who gives me strength. (Phil. 4:11–13)

   Like Paul, Christians live because ultimately they are dependent on nothing and no one except God. They are able to take the bad yet love God and serve others, without hating God or envying the better situations of others.

3. **Really free people live honestly.** They know that they can live in such a fashion because they are honest. Christ's free peo-

ple are honest with God, with themselves, and with others. When they are false, they own up to it. They confess it and continue to live, even when they look like fools. They are willing to look like fools because being really free means that they no longer glorify themselves. They know that their reputation is not supreme. They know that they have been changed, and are being changed. The really free individual wants that change to be complete even if it hurts. He will give up human approval to find Christ's approval.

4. **Really free people are without pretense.** They know that because they are honest, they cannot live with sin and guilt. The really free person sins, but refuses to live with his sin. He refuses to be satisfied with only an image of piety. He may even appear less worthy than those who are not really free because he is so ready to repent of his sin. He will walk alone rather than lose the integrity of his conscience and the purpose for which he was redeemed.

5. **Really free people live today.** They know that yesterday is dead, and that tomorrow may never come on this earth. Now is the time that must be filled with godly living. In this, the Christian somewhat resembles the existentialist. Both appreciate the "now," but only the Christian lives "now" in light of eternity. Thus he can surrender a lifetime of "nows" to save a friend. Today may be the last "now" on earth, but even this can be used freely because it is "not worth comparing with the glory that will be revealed" (Rom. 8:18).

6. **Really free people live without anxiety.** Terror-filled living is gone. They know that worry will not add one moment to their lives (Matt. 6:27). They also know that the choice to be anxious is a conscious step out of today and into the unknown of tomorrow. The really free person knows that living in the tomorrow is an attempt to avoid the duties or the disappointments of today—which would lead to losing the

blessings of today. He knows that Christ is prepared to take our burdens at every moment (Matt. 11:28–30). He knows that to flee to the unknown tomorrow or the well worn-out yesterday is to mock the privilege of being alive today. He will not retreat into yesterday. He will not advance into the future until he has lived today. This moment has been given to delight in—in service and joy—even in the face of trials.

7. **Really free people stand.** The really free person is his own man before God. He often says "No" when it is much easier to say "Yes." He doesn't slavishly depend on others for self-definition or direction. He may seem aloof or indifferent to others, but he is not. It is just that his being part of the Christian body doesn't require him to be a carbon copy of other members, and he resists the pull of complacent conformity. He is not self-sufficient, but he has become so reliant on God that he is freed of extreme dependence on men. In a similar way, he doesn't depend upon the good opinions of men, for he has the approval of God. Of course, God's approval requires that he seek peace with all men wherever possible (Rom. 12:18), but he is not a man-pleaser (Rom. 2:29). This keeps him always a bit out of step with his contemporaries, a bit of a mystery.

8. **Really free people are new.** This person is not someone with new and better skills, nor someone who is armed with new natural potential or new insights. As Paul says, "Therefore, if anyone is in Christ, he is a new creation; the old has gone, the new has come!" (2 Cor. 5:17). We must embrace this reality. To be really free is to be new on a daily basis, moment by moment. Christ's death and resurrection constantly causes us to start new. No confessed sin is held against us; no condemnation lingers from the past. No character flaw need hinder us as we willingly give ourselves over to Christ.

To be really free, then, means that since we are new, the old patterns and practices do not demolish us. In God's sight we are new and perfect in Christ. As a "new creation," the old things that have "passed away" will continue to pass away. We will see victory, because in Christ and His death on our behalf, we are already victorious. Since we are more than conquerors, the really free person knows that it is stupid and sinful to live as less than a conqueror. He simply refuses.

Study Guide

1. Read John 8:36. Now say to yourself, "The Son has set me free, and I am free indeed. I am really free." Is this statement true? Why or why not?

2. Review the eight marks of a really free person. Which of these marks characterize your own life? Which don't?

3. How does the doctrine of "new creation" (2 Cor. 5:17) give us hope and confidence in our struggle for real freedom?

Conclusion

*Y*ou can spend your life hearing Jesus describe your freedom and:

1. Decide that He meant it only for some times.
2. Decide that He meant it only for some.
3. Decide that it costs too much.
4. Decide that you can just never achieve it.
5. Decide to envy those who are really free, as if their freedom was specifically designed to make you feel deprived.

Or:

You can decide to live the life that allows you to be the person God wants you to be. You won't be unmoved or untouched or untroubled. You will simply be unshackled from sin. The work of salvation belongs to God. But you, having been redeemed, can decide whether your life as a Christian will be a mockery of what the Spirit desires for you or a model of biblical joy and freedom. The choice is yours. And God, by His Spirit's power, will assist you every step of the way.

Paul said, "It is for freedom that Christ has set us free. Stand firm, then, and do not let yourselves be burdened again by a yoke of slavery" (Gal. 5:1).

Jesus said, "So if the Son sets you free, *YOU WILL BE REALLY FREE*" (John 8:36).

In choosing Christ, you have chosen freedom. May God grant you the courage to live as those who are *REALLY FREE!*

Study Guide

1. Freedom in Christ grants us many options, including the option to return to slavery. What are some of the decisions you could make to reject real freedom? Which are particularly tempting for you personally?

2. What is God's ultimate purpose for setting you free? How does this purpose energize and empower you to embrace that freedom?

3. The choice is yours: Will you become a mockery of the Spirit's design for your life, or a model of Biblical joy and freedom. How will you live?

About the Author

Dr. Richard L. Ganz practiced clinical psychology and taught at Syracuse University and the Upstate Medical Center complex, before coming to faith in Jesus Christ. He then went on to receive theological training at Westminster Theological Seminary, and worked with Dr. Jay E. Adams at the Christian Counseling and Educational Foundation. He is currently the senior pastor of a growing church in Ottawa, Canada. He is also president of Ottawa Theological Hall, where he teaches biblical counseling. He lectures at universities, seminaries, and churches, and does numerous conferences internationally. He has authored several books including *Psychobabble, The Secret of Self-Control,* and *Twenty Controversies That Almost Killed A Church.*

Breaking Free! is the counseling ministry of Dr. Richard L. Ganz. If you are interested in a *Breaking Free!* seminar (or other biblical counseling seminars) for your local church, you can contact Dr. Ganz at: richganz@storm.ca.

Peacemaker Resources

To order, call 800-338-1445

The Young Peacemaker
By Corlette Sande

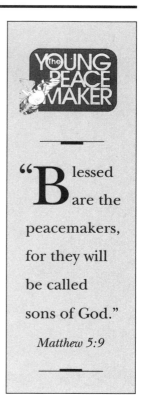

This detailed curriculum deals with the same material as *The Peacemaker*, but is designed for children. *The Young Peacemaker* is designed to teach children to prevent and resolve conflict by applying biblical principals of confession, forgiveness, communication, and character development. The use of realistic stories, practical applications, role plays, and stimulating activities makes this curriculum ideal for 8–12 year olds. Great home school or family resource.

Parent / Teacher Manual
Item # PR02 . . . . *$19.95*

12 Student Activity Books
Item # PR03 . . . . *$13.95*

Manual plus 12 Activity Books
Item # PR04 . . . . *$29.95*

"**B**lessed are the peacemakers, for they will be called sons of God."

Matthew 5:9

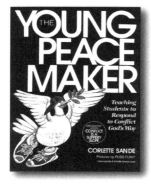

Shepherding a Child's Heart Resources